Here is a marvelous trio of plays to address three scourges of society that plague African Americans today: injustice, demoralization, and despair. Charlotte E. May-Séré utilizes her vast life experience to confront the challenges and heal the wounds of African Americans by planting lost seeds of the African heritage with images and words that speak to the heart. *The Stakes: Three Plays of the Black Experience to Heal, to Train, to Entertain* is a dynamic training vehicle for staff, college students, and clients in the recovery and mental health system. *The Stakes* provides an important and powerful template to counteract discrimination, sexual harassment and addiction-with inspiration, empathy, and hope.

Dr. Sherry Reiter, Director of The Creative "Righting" Center, author of *Writing Away the Demons: Stories of Creative Coping Through Transformative Writing*

To Oteal,
   With warmest
wishes.
      Enjoy!
   Love,
   Charlotte
March 6, 2014

THE STAKES:

Three Plays of the Black Experience

THE STAKES:

Three Plays of the Black Experience
to Heal, to Train, to Entertain

Charlotte E. May-Séré

iUniverse LLC
Bloomington

THE STAKES: THREE PLAYS OF THE BLACK EXPERIENCE TO HEAL, TO TRAIN, TO ENTERTAIN

Copyright © 2013 Charlotte E. May-Séré.

iUniverse books may be ordered through booksellers or by contacting:
iUniverse LLC
1663 Liberty Drive
Bloomington, IN 47403
www.iuniverse.com
1-800-Authors (1-800-288-4677)

ISBN: 978-1-4759-8393-7 (sc)
ISBN: 978-1-4759-8394-4 (hc)
ISBN: 978-1-4759-8395-1 (e)
Library of Congress Control Number: 2013905876

Printed in the United States of America.

iUniverse rev. date: 12/10/2013

In Memoriam

In loving memory of my parents, the late
Dr. Percy C. and Edna M. May

"Yes, and there were the rituals … through which our people had imposed order upon the chaos of their lives."

"Bearden" in *The Collected Essays of Ralph Ellison*, edited by John F. Callahan

Contents

In Memoriam vii

Author's Preface xiii

Acknowledgments xvii

Introduction xix

The Stakes 1
    Act One 3
    Act Two 43

Abiona 79
    Scene One 81
    Scene Two 97
    Scene Three 107

GumBO 117

About the Author 159

Author's Preface

The Stakes: Three Plays of the Black Experience to Heal, to Train, to Entertain grew in part from my career experience as a social worker of African descent, and in part from my fascination with the imaginative use of the written word. Ideas in the plays are examined from the vantage points of societal challenges, workplace dynamics, and African roots. In my career experience, working with clients grappling with major challenges such as addictions, poverty, and mental illness was a daily task. And workplace dynamics was a constant in my career; out of necessity, continual exchange with colleagues and co-workers formed an essential part of the experience.

My interest in using an African roots motif in the plays stems of course from my being of African descent, with life experiences representative of the proscription that often oppresses persons of African descent in the United States. Additionally, as a social worker, I searched for ways to address the demoralization of my clients and to shore up their resolve; many were African American and victimized with a myriad of social ills, often including racial injustice. Moreover, using the African roots motif was a way of exploring applications of the old-world mythology and culture of the African tradition to current social challenges.

The title of the collection, *The Stakes*, refers to both the title of the entire three-play collection as well as to the title of the first play in the group. Dictionary definitions refer to "stakes" as prizes, and that which is "at stake" is that which is at risk or that which is hazarded. All three plays feature stakes relating to the self-image and the self-efficacy of human beings yearning to live in a world free of prejudice, addictions, mental illness, and other societal ills that compromise authenticity. The stakes are therefore those elements of authenticity risked when the individual fails to courageously challenge threats to that which is at the fundamental core of his or her being.

The impetus for the play *The Stakes* arose from several of my own experiences as a female African American staff member in an employee population composed of a minority of individuals of African descent, where, especially, very few administrators were of African descent. Often there was a feeling of being in the midst of a milieu encompassing not only racial inequities, but also sexual harassment and office politics. Having personally experienced the damaging effects of these phenomena and having observed the damaging effects on victims and perpetrators alike, I looked to the rich African folkloric culture for healing energies.

Abiona grew from my work in counseling clients who were mentally ill and often also addicted to harmful substances. Backsliding after firm resolve was frequent in the struggle to overcome a dangerous and addictive way of living, and this lifestyle was usually complicated and exacerbated by a concomitant psychiatric illness. It was also frequently observed in this client population that even when a serious addiction was present in both partners of a relationship, often only one partner sought a cure for the addiction. Often clients had difficulty recognizing the conflict and expected that the twosome could continue without change, despite the obvious clash in values arising when the partners did not agree on the use of addictive substances. Of course the counseling focus in those cases was to help the partners recognize and come to terms with the conflict.

GumBO also stemmed from my experience of counseling clients with serious addictions to harmful substances. The play presents a situation where three clients in residential treatment, apparently committed to abstinence from illegal substances, are left on their own without counselor support and must deal with the challenge occurring when one of the three is tempted to resume abuse of illegal drugs. In my career experience, many of my clients entered addictions treatment and recovery programs, and many of them had some traits in common with the characters in *GumBO*.

The Stakes: Three Plays of the Black Experience to Heal, to Train, to Entertain can therefore be viewed as an exploration of African roots as a link in the healing fabric for challenges of addictions, psychiatric illness, sexual harassment, racial injustice, and the many complexities attending those ills. Because much of the misery experienced by persons of African descent is related to that very descent, it seems fitting that the wealth and beauty of their African roots should form a part of the healing. This collection also seeks to examine the application of an African roots motif to the many other pains often occurring with, and in addition to, racial inequities.

Acknowledgments

My many thanks go to my siblings, P. Conrad May and Nancy J. May, for their warm counsel and encouragement. My daughter Moronké Ayorémi Séré has shown immense patience and understanding, as navigating the waters of this collection has left me with decreased time for family togetherness.

I extend my deep appreciation to Sherry Reiter, author of Writing Away the Demons: Stories of Creative Coping Through Transformative Writing. She kindly read every word of the manuscript of this book, and offered warm encouragement.

My myriad career experiences over the course of many years are the soil out of which many of the ideas for these plays grew, and this book is indebted to all those experiences, including the painful ones.

In gathering proverbs for use in *The Stakes*, certain books and journals were of invaluable help. Included among these are Charlotte and Wolf Leslau's *African Proverbs*; Vanessa Cross's *An Anthology of Black Folk Wit, Wisdom, and Sayings*; Julia Stewart's *African Proverbs and Wisdom*; Deborah Day's *Mindful Messages*; R. Sutherland Rattray's *Ashanti Proverbs*; and the *African Studies* periodicals of 1944 and 1947.

The Complete Pelican Shakespeare, Webster's New World Dictionary, and Homer's *The Iliad* were helpful in the structuring of *GumBO*. In selecting the Yoruba name "Abiona," books of benefit were R. C. Abraham's *Dictionary of Modern Yoruba*, and E. C. Rowlands's *Yoruba*.

Also contributing to the inspiration required to complete this work are Joanne and Elmer Martin's *Social Work and the Black Experience*; Wole Soyinka's *Myth, Literature, and the African World*; Thandeka's

Learning to be White; John F. Callahan's (ed.) *The Collected Essays of Ralph Ellison;* and Dan Poynter's *The Self-Publishing Manual.*

Guidance in the techniques of the craft of playwriting came from Sam Smiley's *Playwriting the Structure of Action.*

Thanks go to my former husband, Edward Adékunle Séré, for his suggestions relative to the Yoruba name of "Abiona." And I gratefully acknowledge the many performing artists who, over the course of readings and full productions of these plays, joined me in making them come alive on stage, and thereby supported the necessary revisions. A special thanks goes to actress Felisha McNeal for contributions she made when she directed a production of *Abiona.*

And many, many thanks, of course, to iUniverse for working with me to cast the manuscript into book form.

Introduction

How to Use These Plays
or
Wouldn't You Rather Heal, Train, and
Entertain All with the Same Stroke?

Adding to their great entertainment value (including holiday entertainment), the plays in *The Stakes: Three Plays of the Black Experience to Heal, to Train, to Entertain* are useful for training of professional persons; for treatment of clients; for performance by college and community theater groups; for literature classes; and for special celebrations.

Training of Professional Staff

The Stakes, the first play in the collection, was successfully presented before a general audience purely for its entertainment value. But the play is well suited for the training of professional persons charged with improving staff-to-staff and staff-to-management relations. Problems raised in *The Stakes* include institutional racial injustice and focus on the psychological origins of racist attitudes. Also raised is the matter of sexual harassment and how it may be enmeshed with racial injustice. In addition, the institutional complaint mechanism may need addressing. Those wishing to work on matters pertaining to institutional racism and problems in the institutional complaint mechanism may well find *The Stakes* a point of departure for the venture. Depicted in that play are staff members victimized by racial prejudice, institutional politics, and sexual harassment. The play could be a starting-off point for agencies seeking to better understand and deal with those and similar matters.

Both *The Stakes* and *Abiona* explore workplace tensions and present the various ways they are resolved within the dramatic structure. Examined are interactions among staff, as well as staff-client interactions.

Abiona and *GumBO*, related one-acts, have immense value for training of health professionals in addition to use of the plays in conjunction with client counseling. *Abiona*, with extensive depictions of staff interacting with clients, offers copious material for teaching and for exploration of various ways of approaching client problems. In *GumBO*, set at a residential addictions treatment center where most interactions are among clients, the influence of a counselor who happens not to be present is clearly palpable. The reason for this is that the clients enact a treatment technique learned from their counselor and appear to benefit from it. This enactment would offer learning opportunities for treatment staff viewing it.

Abiona has been presented at seminars for training of health-care professionals including social workers, psychologists, psychiatrists, nurses, medical students, and other health-care staff. The training program included introductory remarks, followed by a play performance before a plenary audience, and finally, breaking into small groups for discussion. Each small group was led by a trained health-care professional with a list of prepared questions to get discussion under way, but with the understanding that discussion was not to be limited to the questions used to start off discussion. A segment of the discussion time was set aside where participants could focus on related matters triggered in their minds by the viewing of the plays, though not necessarily in the plays. Following the small-group discussion sessions there was return to the plenary group, with each small group having chosen one person from the small group to appear on a panel moderated by one of the seminar planners. Each chosen representative presented the salient ideas of his or her group, followed by plenary group discussion. At one seminar, the panel presentation was followed by an expert in mental health and addictions who spoke to the group, further elaborating on issues raised by the panel. This was the format for the *Abiona* training seminar. *The Stakes* and *GumBO* could be used similarly in seminars for staff training.

Treatment of Clients

The two related one-acts, *Abiona* and *GumBO*, can be performed before client populations in conjunction with client treatment programs. The plays may be performed by a community theater group, then viewed by clients, followed by small-group counseling, with focus on matters raised in the plays as well as related matters arising in clients' minds that were triggered by the play viewing—though not necessarily directly related to ideas in the play. Of course each small group would be led by a trained health-care professional. In some instances, clients themselves may perform the plays with the help of a facilitator in conjunction with their treatment. Individual counseling might also be combined with the play viewing. There are many possibilities for staff and client creativity in use of the plays for effective treatment.

All three plays depict clients up against problems that confront many real-life clients. In *The Stakes*, client James Tulane, recuperating from a catastrophic physical illness, is confronted with financial issues that threaten to derail him. Clients Eedie and Bo of *Abiona* and *GumBO* are challenged by their addictions, HIV, and their histories of illegal activities. All clients in the plays have the benefit of professional staff members who attempt to engage them in amelioration of the various social challenges confronting them. The plays are highly applicable to the field of bibliotherapy, including drama therapy.

Literary Study

The Stakes: Three Plays of the Black Experience to Heal, to Train, to Entertain offers works that illustrate the use of symbolism, metaphor, and imagery, and the plays contain allusions to classical references.

In *The Stakes*, the name for the new activity center founded by Victoria is Healing Hands; it echoes the idea of the hands of her client, Tulane, who sculpts, and who has created a sculpture of clasping hands.

The hands symbol relates also to the hands of surgeon Curtis Wyman who healed Tulane through surgery, and symbolically to Victoria's reaching out to Tulane. Moreover, the hands symbol points to the idea of racial healing. Tulane says he created hands of differing hues because at Healing Hands "all colors will create hand-in-hand." Surgeon Curtis Wyman seeks inspiration from the wisdom of ancient African proverbs as he navigates the racism and politics of the institution that employs him. Some of the proverbs have metaphorical force, as in "When the music changes, so should the dance!" a proverb he recites in an effort to warn his coworker, Victoria, of sinister activities in her milieu.

Eedie of *Abiona* uses a running metaphor in her assertion that her old name reminds her of the time when "I was in a fog at the back of the pack." And later she says, "I've passed milestones. Now's time to surge to the finish line." Obviously here running works as a symbol because in the play it suggests aspiration as well as the idea of actual, physical running. Use of the symbol provides an image on the one hand; on the other, it carries the development of the character, since a passion for running track is one quality Eedie possesses. But it also brings out another quality: her deep aspiration to rescue her life from the old one of abusing drugs and concomitantly engaging in other illegal activities. Aspects of the sport of running are also employed in the language of other characters in *Abiona*, with literal as well as symbolic use.

In *GumBO*, bee imagery is employed in the metaphorical exchange between Bo and Minnie, when Bo links his inclination to use cocaine as a seeking of honey. Minnie retorts, "What about the bees?" Minnie responds similarly when Bo questions why his former girlfriend left him. Reminding him of the intransigence of the addiction he had at the time, she says, "You had bees in your brains." Hence the extended bee metaphor serves to bring out Bo's intransigence and how it interferes with his relationships. Bo's assertions point to certain character traits he possesses, and Minnie's response works to build her character portrayal. This dialogue foreshadows plot development, preparing the audience or reader for subsequent action in the play. Similar use is made of other symbols in *GumBO*, especially the mirror symbolism, the use of symbolic language preparing for the subsequent heightening of conflict among the characters.

Moreover, the plays contain references to other classical proverbs, legends, myths, and tropes. In *The Stakes*, ancient African proverbs help build the character Curtis Wyman. In *Abiona*, the ancient legend of West African god Ogun looms over much of the dramatic activity. In the idea of mirroring in *GumBO*, there is reference to a scene from Shakespeare's *Hamlet*. In the idea of shoring up resolve, reference is made to a scene from Homer's *The Iliad*.

College and Community Theater Groups

The issues dealt with in the plays make the pieces especially suitable for performance by college and community theater groups. Addictions, mental illness, institutional politics, sexual harassment, and racial injustice—continual societal challenges that confront the lives of many—call for ongoing dialogue in the search for solutions. Also, literary references in the plays would correlate with ongoing literature study occurring at the college level. Moreover, all three plays address the idea of African roots, relating them to immediate challenges in the Western world. *The Stakes: Three Plays of the Black Experience to Heal, to Train, to Entertain* encourages dialogue that should help to bring concerns about the issues out into the open where they can be properly grappled with, with steps taken to begin to surmount them.

Use of the Plays for Holiday Celebrations

All of the plays are suitable for performance at any time of the year. Yet it is also true that any and all of the plays may be used as part of a holiday or special-event commemoration.

All three plays are highly suited for performance during Black History Month. Characters in all plays of this collection employ ideas of African roots in attempting to address the major challenges before them. Surgeon Curtis Wyman of *The Stakes* collects African proverbs for inspiration as he navigates the politics and racism systematized in the institution where he works. He deftly responds to the insensitivity of colleagues with apt proverbs. Most notably, he employs African proverbs in the many passages where he shows warmth and encouragement toward his beleaguered co-worker, Victoria. For example, when she is threatened with being forced from her job, he proverbially counsels her to fight and press to the end in order to be victorious.

Eedie, the protagonist in *Abiona,* seeks a new name to ransom herself from her previous life of drug addiction and prostitution, and she relates this desire to the African practice of naming a child according to what was happening at the time of its birth. In addition, she calls upon the legend of the West African god Ogun as a source of support as she reaches for a new life. Referring to her desire to choose a new name to symbolize the positive changes in her life she says, "I'm startin' a new life. It's somethin' like gettin' born." Moreover, she identifies with Ogun, with whom she shares addictive weaknesses. But Ogun is also Lord of the Road, so because Eedie is a runner, her reverence and identification with the god are increased, and thereby her motivation for improving her life is enhanced as well. Hence the African roots idea prepares the ground for further plot and character development. The subsequent action grows out of Eedie's early focus on African roots, from which she receives leverage for her desire to change her life.

GumBO protagonist Bo is excited to learn that the word "gumbo" derives from an African language word meaning "okra." And he later distills from the Bantu roots of the word an application that may support his desire to free himself from a cycle of addiction. He says, "Bo's gonna show how he can stick with it—be as sticky as okra ..."

And all three plays would certainly heighten any program in celebration of Social Work Month. Characters in the plays representing persons challenged by illness, addictions, racial disharmony, and institutional politics manifest situations that cry out for wise counsel. *Abiona* was successfully presented in dramatic reading format at a National Association of Social Workers Illinois Conference. In addition, performances of *Abiona* and *GumBO,* containing references to addictions and HIV/AIDS, would enhance events in recognition of Addictions Treatment Month and HIV/AIDS Month. All three plays, containing important poetic sequences, are also suitable for performance to highlight Poetry Month. Both *Abiona* and *GumBO* have been presented at the Conference of the National Association of Poetry Therapy.

GumBO is especially relevant for holiday use, since there is a holiday motif in the play. It would do well performed in conjunction with almost any holiday, but might work especially well with Thanksgiving, Christmas, and Kwanzaa.

Thus, any event planned at any time of the year would be enhanced by inclusion of drama from the collection *The Stakes: Three Plays of the Black Experience to Heal, to Train, to Entertain.*

The Stakes

A Play in Two Acts

CHARACTERS
(In Order of Appearance)

VICTORIA SHEPHERD.....twenty-three, a social worker, African American

WINNIE.. twenty-five, a nurse, Caucasian American

RANDALL RANSOM................ thirty-two, a physician, Caucasian American

MRS. SIMMONS.....................................fifty, a social worker, African American

JAMES TULANE .... eighty-two, a patient, Caucasian American

CURTIS WYMAN................................. sixty-two, a surgeon, African American

AGNES DUDWORTH...........................fifty, a supervisor, Caucasian American

HAZEL HUFF.. fifty, a physician, Caucasian American

1st EMPLOYEE........................fifty, a hospital staff member, African American

2nd EMPLOYEE ....fifty, a hospital staff member, Caucasian American

CLIENTS of various ages and sexes

THE STAKES

THE TIME
The present

THE PLACE
Offices, corridors, and conference room of a large
general hospital, anywhere in the United States

SYNOPSIS OF ACTS

ACT I
Morning

ACT II
Afternoon

ACT ONE

SCENE I

SETTING:

A clinic examining room. The room contains an examining table and chair, plus a sink with soap and paper towels. Next to the examining room is a conference room with podium. A bunch of dried flowers is on a shelf there. In the background is VICTORIA's office, which may be on an elevated structure. It contains a desk and two chairs. Next to it is the office of her supervisor, AGNES DUDWORTH.

AT RISE:

VICTORIA is in her office working with papers as well as on the telephone. She is an attractive young lady, with a warm, friendly demeanor. She is genuinely invested in helping her clients and in being of value to the institution that employs her.

WINNIE enters the examining room. She is petite and shapely and walks somewhat seductively. She arranges things, then leaves the scene. She returns almost immediately with a broom and dustpan and sweeps the conference room and examining room. She leaves the broom and dustpan in the conference room when she goes out again. She returns immediately with charts, which she deposits on the table in the conference room, and then leaves.

RANDALL RANSOM enters the conference room by a door different from the one WINNIE exited by. He is a handsome man, about medium height. He has a slightly rakish look, together with a certain self-absorbed arrogance. He picks up a chart and begins to read it. He then reads from other charts and makes notes in some of them.

VICTORIA greets her colleague, MRS. SIMMONS, who is just entering VICTORIA's office. MRS. SIMMONS is matronly and has a warm, friendly demeanor. She holds a box of faux pearls that she gives to VICTORIA.

MRS. SIMMONS. Faux pearls for the jewelry class. I'm donating them to the Center.

VICTORIA, *accepting the box of pearls.* Dear Mrs. Simmons! Thank you, thank you, thank you! Faux pearls for the jewelry class! I'll take them to the conference room where we're keeping things for the Center.

MRS. SIMMONS. Don't thank me, Ms. Shepherd! You're the one who deserves thanks. You're the founder. Imagine! Organized the Center all on your own! How could you accomplish so much?

VICTORIA. Giving others a chance to create!

MRS. SIMMONS. You give your *heart!*

VICTORIA. Ah! To go down deep and raise those hidden treasures!

MRS. SIMMONS. *(Noticing book on VICTORIA's desk, she reads the title.) African Proverbs.*

VICTORIA. That book was donated for the African proverb class.

MRS. SIMMONS. A class on African proverbs! Who's leading it?

VICTORIA. Our very own Dr. Curtis Wyman!

MRS. SIMMONS. Dr. Wyman? The *surgeon?*

VICTORIA. The *surgeon* Dr. Wyman! Proverbs! The perfect flesh for his surgeon's mind. He's even *writing* about the proverbs.

MRS. SIMMONS. He's perfect for the proverb class! There's such a buzz about the Center! Hear it's called Healing Hands.

VICTORIA. Healing Hands. Yes, that's the name for the Center.

MRS. SIMMONS. Excellent name! *(Notices box of modeling clay.)* But what about this clay?

VICTORIA. Modeling clay for the sculpture class.

MRS. SIMMONS. Sculpture? Can't think of a soul to run a sculpture class!

VICTORIA. None other than our good client, Mr. Tulane!

MRS. SIMMONS. Mr. Tulane! But I thought he—

VICTORIA. Wait till you see him!

MRS. SIMMONS. So he's better! Wonderful! Of course it's a credit to his doctors—especially Dr. Wyman. But credit also goes to you. Think I didn't notice how much time you spent? How *patient* you were?

VICTORIA. You always encourage me, Mrs. Simmons. With Mr. Tulane, with the Center, with whatever I do!

MRS. SIMMONS. My pleasure. But I'll be leaving shortly. Today's a clinic day. I bet Mr. Tulane'll stop to see you.

VICTORIA. He needs those funds.

MRS. SIMMONS. Those funds. I'm sure Mr. Tulane wants to see you *bad*. But before I go, now, I just have to say it— *(Hesitates.)*

VICTORIA. What's on your mind, Mrs. Simmons?

MRS. SIMMONS. Beware of that Ransom guy! *(Indicates conference room where RANDALL is at this moment.)*

VICTORIA. Dr. Ransom.

MRS. SIMMONS. Him! Dr. Ransom! Struts around here like he's chief cock in a bunch of hens. Steady getting an IV feed. Guess what's in the IV bag.

VICTORIA. I can't guess. What's in his IV bag?

MRS. SIMMONS. Himself. Full of himself! Don't *ever* turn your back!

VICTORIA. My supervisor, Ms. Dudworth, told him not to be so *loose* around me.

MRS. SIMMONS. Did it do any good?

VICTORIA. Can't tell yet.

MRS. SIMMONS. The way he is with *us*, if you know what I mean!

VICTORIA. We're all human beings.

MRS. SIMMONS. *He* makes differences!

VICTORIA. Dr. Ransom is a pocketful of problems. But Ms. Dudworth helps so much. I don't worry.

MRS. SIMMONS. Still, you watch the man. Where *we're* concerned. But he'd still like to get *in* with a pretty young lady! (*There is a knock at the door.*)

VICTORIA. Mr. Tulane.

MRS. SIMMONS. I understand, dear. But mark my word. Watch that Ransom fellow. Promise me.

VICTORIA. Thank you, Mrs. Simmons. I promise. (*MRS. SIMMONS greets TULANE as she is leaving and ushers him in to see VICTORIA. TULANE walks with a cane. His voice is cheerful and shows that he is confident he is on the mend. He holds behind his back a gift for VICTORIA.*)

TULANE. Something for Miss Vicky!

VICTORIA. No gifts for me, Mr. Tulane.

TULANE. But I made it myself!

VICTORIA. What could it be? (*TULANE reveals his gift, a clay paperweight in the shape of three clasping hands, one jet black, one white, and one a shade of yellowish beige.*) A paperweight!

TULANE. A paperweight for the weightless Miss Vicky! She walks on air!

VICTORIA. Three clasping hands! How lovely!

TULANE. With the Center named Healing Hands, I knew what to make for you. Hands.

VICTORIA. Three hands, clasping: a black hand, a yellow hand, a white hand.

7

TULANE. Because at Healing Hands, all colors will create hand-in-hand.

VICTORIA. Thank you, Mr. Tulane. This will be our symbol. It will occupy a special, central place at our center.

TULANE. But these hands also stand for how you reached out to me, through the darkness.

VICTORIA. That's why I'm here, Mr. Tulane.

TULANE. The paperweight stands for the great weight on your shoulders. Yet you carry it all as if it were paper.

VICTORIA. You give me too much credit, Mr. Tulane. Volunteers make Healing Hands. And thank heavens *you're* leading the sculpting class!

TULANE. Know why I'm for the sculpting class?

VICTORIA. You enjoy sculpting and wish to share it with others.

TULANE. But I sculpt because of you, Miss Vicky. You put that idea here.

VICTORIA. Sculpting was to brighten your outlook.

TULANE. Just when I gave up on life, you wanted me to celebrate life! Shape the shapeless clay!

VICTORIA. You were more at ease.

TULANE. You made ease out of "disease." Sculpting is a prayer for me, a paperweight for you.

VICTORIA. A lovely gift, Mr. Tulane. Thank you. *(Pause.)*

TULANE. You're welcome, Miss Vicky. I'll be getting along now. Isn't it time when you go down there to work on charts?

VICTORIA. Yes, I'll be leaving shortly. But before we go, have you received a letter from that fund we applied to?

TULANE. No word yet, Miss Vicky.

VICTORIA. Any day now you should hear something.

TULANE. After clinic, if there's a letter, I'll come right back so you can see it.

VICTORIA. By all means, Mr. Tulane. Let's stay right with this until you get those funds you so deserve.

TULANE. Sure thing, Miss Vicky. If there's a letter, I'll bring it right to you. *(TULANE leaves VICTORIA's office, exits the scene. VICTORIA gathers up the book, the box of modeling clay, and the box of faux pearls. She walks to the conference room and enters.)*

VICTORIA. Good morning, Dr. Ransom. *(She puts the book, faux pearls, and modeling clay on a shelf next to the dried flowers.)*

RANDALL. *Good* morning? No, it's a *beautiful* morning, a beautiful day!

VICTORIA. Why yes, it is a beautiful day.

RANDALL. And here you come looking just *like* the day!

VICTORIA, *ignoring the compliment.* I have some charts to review.

RANDALL, *slightly huffed, but not entirely put off.* Any one in particular?

VICTORIA. I'll start with James Tulane.

RANDALL, *handing VICTORIA the chart.* James Tulane. What's going on with him?

VICTORIA. He's improved. But he still needs the State to pay more of his expenses.

RANDALL. Well? What's being done for the man?

VICTORIA. We helped him obtain more in his food allowance. He was using his food money to pay on his medical bills. Then we helped him apply to the Special Fund.

RANDALL. What else?

VICTORIA. Most importantly, we treated his depression. That, plus counseling and monetary assistance changed his whole outlook. He's cheerful now!

RANDALL. But he still needs more. Right?

VICTORIA. Of course, and we're in the process of—

RANDALL. So what you *did*, didn't really *do* it, huh?

VICTORIA. We helped in many ways. Ms. Dudworth can vouch for that. We dispensed to him from our Service Fund. He doesn't qualify for more help from the State because of the income standard, and then, too—

RANDALL, *cutting her off.* I see, I see. Well! (*He eyes her up and down, a look of dalliance coming over him.*) Let's talk about *us*, huh?

VICTORIA. Excuse me?

RANDALL. You look better and better every day. *(Pause.)* Know that?

VICTORIA. Now really, Dr. Ransom—

RANDALL. Randall. How many times must I tell you? Call me Randall!

VICTORIA. But how many times must I tell *you*—

RANDALL. Relax.

VICTORIA. Relax? How can I, when you're constantly—

RANDALL. I told you how things are with my wife and me.

VICTORIA. But still—

RANDALL. Understand. I've been with my wife for years. We have children. But it doesn't mean ...

VICTORIA. Yes?

RANDALL. It's like chemistry—the chemistry I studied so long ago. Chemistry. You mix hydrogen and sulphur. No matter how often. No matter when you mix 'em. You get the same result each time. Hydrogen sulfide. Every time you mix 'em it's hydrogen sulfide! *(He simulates a look of revulsion, fans the air to get rid of the rotten-egg smell of hydrogen sulfide.)*

VICTORIA. Then get help.

RANDALL, *exasperated.* You should be intelligent enough to understand.

VICTORIA. What could there be to understand?

RANDALL. You don't get it!

VICTORIA. There's nothing to get!

RANDALL. Get this: smart guys are restless.

VICTORIA. That has nothing to do with me.

RANDALL. A man gets restless. He has to keep looking.

VICTORIA. Not this way.

RANDALL. Women are flattered with a guy like me.

VICTORIA, *completely turned off.* If you'll excuse me. This is a busy morning ... *(She sits down and begins to write in a chart.)* Service sheets in these charts. After that, final plans for the Healing Hands Center.

RANDALL. Your center, your Healing Hands Center, is just another program when there are already too many programs.

VICTORIA. But none like this! At Healing Hands clients will bring out the specialness just waiting to be stirred and mixed, then spread on canvas to make something new and lovely. All are included. Illness is no barrier. Guidance for budding artists, yearning writers, aspiring dancers, theater—

RANDALL. You name it, huh? You and your Healing Hands have the answer! Well, let me tell you: It takes more than an idea. It takes *money.* Money!

VICTORIA. Lots of donations. Today, faux pearls for the jewelry class. Yesterday, clay for Mr. Tulane's sculpting class. And look, someone's donated dried flowers for the floral class!

RANDALL. Stuff! A few donations. So? Staff must be hired!

VICTORIA. The great thing about it—

RANDALL. Nothing great about it! Pick us clean, hiring staff we can't afford!

VICTORIA. But *volunteers* will run Healing Hands.

RANDALL. What? Think people'll work for free?

VICTORIA. Volunteers are eager to join Healing Hands.

RANDALL. They won't show up!

VICTORIA. There's even a waiting list of volunteers. People are eager to share their hearts. *(RANDALL is uncomfortable, squirms, doesn't know what else to say to deprecate Healing Hands.)*

RANDALL. Then share your heart with me, you great big chocolate drop! *(He pinches her playfully on the cheek.)*

VICTORIA, *moving away from him.* Keep your hands off me! And don't call me "chocolate drop"!

RANDALL. But chocolate drops are sweet when they know their place! *(He makes lip movements to demonstrate.)*

VICTORIA. Don't call me "chocolate drop"!

RANDALL. Sorry. *(Pause.)* But what about *me?* I need a little attention. *(Pause. He places his hand on her knee.)* Wouldn't you say?

VICTORIA. Don't touch me! *(Immediately gets up and moves toward the door.)*

RANDALL. (*Rushes ahead of her, gets to the door, and blocks it so she can't get out.*) Just tell me what you like.

VICTORIA, *struggling to get the door open.* Let me out! Let me out!

RANDALL. Tell me what you *like.* (*He continues blocking the door with his back and one hand, and tries to paw her with his other hand. She fends him off as best she can while trying to get away.*)

VICTORIA. To *leave!*

RANDALL. There's a button here somewhere ...

VICTORIA, *trying to get past RANDALL. Please,* Dr. Ransom ...

RANDALL. There's a button here somewhere ... (*Continues trying to paw her.*)

VICTORIA. Let me out!

RANDALL. Just tell me what you *like.* I'm very amenable.

VICTORIA. Let me out! (*VICTORIA struggles furiously trying to get past RANDALL. He finally reluctantly moves aside. She rushes out. RANDALL makes angry gestures of irritation, then collects his composure and resumes reading of chart. WINNIE enters by same door VICTORIA just exited from. She bustles in, carrying supplies for the examining room, and distributes these with assistance from RANDALL.*)

WINNIE. Why, that little twit! Zipped past me without a word! Could see I was all loaded down. She—

RANDALL, *innocently.* Who, sweetheart?

WINNIE. That little spittoon!

RANDALL. Who?

WINNIE. That Victoria Shepherd.

RANDALL. Victoria Shepherd? Let's see … ah, yes!

WINNIE. What's her *problem*? Almost bumped me over!

RANDALL, *sympathetic toward WINNIE.* Hellcat!

WINNIE. What *is* her trouble?!

RANDALL. Vixen!

WINNIE. Running past me like that, almost knocked me down. Why, she— Why, that—

RANDALL. Don't worry your pretty head about these brain-free staffers.

WINNIE. A no-brain who thinks she's *so* competent! She's spoiling the clients. Helping this one with more income, that one over his depression. To say nothing of her Committee for the Indigent! And that Healing Hands—

RANDALL. Oh, how we go on about that little drop!

WINNIE. What was she *scared* about?

RANDALL. Who knows?! They scare easily, and do they run! When they're scared, all you can see are the whites of their eyes! *(Laughs.)*

WINNIE. *Scared.* As if something just happened. As if something happened … *here! (Pause. RANDALL is silent.)* What happened, Randall? Was somebody hollering?

RANDALL. Wasn't from here.

WINNIE. Something happened *here*. *(Pause.)*

RANDALL. I wasn't going to say anything.

WINNIE. Tell me. What happened?

RANDALL. They're always after men of power.

WINNIE. Why, that brazen little—

RANDALL. Don't worry, honey. I can handle it.

WINNIE. Can you?

RANDALL. She was on me like a louse. Wouldn't keep her hands off me.

WINNIE. What?

RANDALL. I told her that between her and me it's strictly business. *(Pause.)*

WINNIE, *enraged.* Why, that—

RANDALL. Don't clutter your mind with inkwells!

WINNIE. Why, the presumptuous little—

RANDALL. Think no more about it. Your big *huggy* bear's here. *(Tries to embrace WINNIE.)*

WINNIE, *coldly.* If he's here, I should hope so.

RANDALL. Here with his arms wide open.

WINNIE, *cold, angry, sarcastic.* I hope so.

RANDALL. Hope no more!

WINNIE. I certainly hope so—after I waited for you till midnight!

RANDALL. You *did?*

WINNIE. And in the *rain!*

RANDALL. Really?

WINNIE. Oh, Randall! Where *were* you?

RANDALL. We were supposed to meet?

WINNIE. How *could* you?

RANDALL. I forgot. *(Pause.)* Now look, Winnie, I'm really sorry. I just forgot.

WINNIE. That's all I ever hear: you just forgot!

RANDALL. Dearest Winnie, I am so sorry. I ... I ... What can I say? I just forgot.

WINNIE. You just forgot. Is that all you can say, after I got soaking wet?

RANDALL. I forgot. You see my ... uh ... *(stammering)* ... my ... my wife ...

WINNIE. Your wife! Your wife! Always your wife! Sometimes I wonder why I—

RANDALL. I'm really sorry, darling.

WINNIE. This always happens.

RANDALL. Now you know how I feel.

WINNIE. But … but … (*RANDALL interrupts her with a passionate kiss. WINNIE melts in his embrace, her body responding with sensuous titillation.*)

RANDALL. Same time, same place?

WINNIE. Same time, same place. Bye, honey! (*WINNIE leaves. RANDALL slaps her on the behind as she's leaving; then he occupies himself again with reading charts. DR. CURTIS WYMAN enters. He is about sixty-two years old. He is a kind, gentle man, compassionate with his patients, sincere with his colleagues. But he has no illusions about the milieu he works in and makes no pretense to the contrary. In his hands are X-rays that he wants to show RANDALL.*)

CURTIS, *holding up X-ray photos.* Hey, Randall, take a look! (*Pause.*) What do you say, Randy?

RANDALL. Huh?

CURTIS. Tulane's. Clean! All clear!

RANDALL. Eh … well.

CURTIS. Randy, these are Tulane's. *Tulane's.* Like I said, cl—

RANDALL. Uh, yes, Tulane, James Tulane. He's improving …

CURTIS. But you didn't see these. You have to see—

RANDALL. Look, Curtis, can we talk about it later?

CURTIS, *puzzled.* Later? Well, sure, but—

RANDALL. Right now something's on my mind.

CURTIS. Something's happening?

RANDALL. Our new employee. What's your opinion?

CURTIS. Several were hired recently. Which one?

RANDALL. The one on Tumor Service.

CURTIS. Ms. Shepherd? Victoria Shepherd?

RANDALL. Victoria Shepherd.

CURTIS. She's competent, and—

RANDALL. *Seems* competent. Anyone can seem competent. We need staff who know what they're doing.

CURTIS. But I said she's competent.

RANDALL. *Seems* competent. *Seems.* A malignant tumor may *seem* like a clump of normal cells until its true nature is revealed.

CURTIS. But—

RANDALL. *Seems.* Perhaps she *seems* competent. That doesn't mean she *is!*

CURTIS. But she's very diligent with our patients. Best of all, she started the Healing Hands Center.

RANDALL. Hog swill! Her Healing Hands gives you a chance to spout your proverbs.

CURTIS. I'm glad to teach African proverbs. I'm pleased to support Healing Hands.

RANDALL. Only the weak need your proverbs. I have no use for them whatsoever. Now what do you say to *that*?

CURTIS. "He who is inflated bursts into pieces."[1]

RANDALL. Your sleazy adages are wasted on me! I'd answer you smartly, but Victoria Shepherd is the topic, in case you forgot. Victoria Shepherd is the topic. And I am not pleased.

CURTIS. Ms. Shepherd gets along with other people.

RANDALL. I know one whose opinion about Victoria Shepherd counts. One in particular.

CURTIS. You have someone in mind.

RANDALL. Agnes Dudworth, her supervisor.

CURTIS. Ms. Dudworth would have a complaint?

RANDALL. I know Agnes Dudworth better than you. *(Pause.)* A chair is vacant.

CURTIS. So Ms. Dudworth wants it.

RANDALL. She smells it; she can almost taste it! But she and our colleague Dr. Hazel Huff are vying for it.

CURTIS. Vying for the chair. Dr. Huff is looking to move up.

RANDALL. Hazel Huff has ties to the hospital board. The board's choice will bear weight in the ultimate appointment.

CURTIS. Of course. But what has all this to do with Ms. Shepherd's job?

RANDALL. My father-in-law is a friend of the hospital president.

CURTIS. Of course. I'm aware of that.

RANDALL. The president and my father-in-law play chess.

CURTIS. But I still don't see—

RANDALL. Agnes Dudworth is looking to her own future. And her future hangs on her department. She won't stand for daffodilling.

CURTIS. Daffodilling? Victoria Shepherd?

RANDALL. All I'm saying is, we have much work to do. And we need staff with, uh, more …

CURTIS. More what?

RANDALL. Why, more, uh, force, I guess. That's it: more force.

CURTIS. (Laughs ironically.) Know what I guess?

RANDALL, angry with CURTIS, vehement. Now get what I'm saying. Victoria Shepherd does not deliver services!

CURTIS. Services?

RANDALL. That's right. A problem delivering services.

CURTIS, laughing, Which ones?

RANDALL, *very irritated.* Which *ones*?! Which *ones*?! *(Immediately after RANDALL's response, JAMES TULANE is shown in by WINNIE, who exits immediately thereafter.)*

CURTIS, *warmly.* Well! Here comes our first patient, our prize patient! How *are* you, Mr. Tulane?

TULANE. Much better, thank you, Doctor, much better.

CURTIS. All clear! Look! *(Shows TULANE his X-ray.)*

TULANE. That's a powerful relief. But Dr. Wyman, it was you who took out the tumor. You got me clear of it.

CURTIS. Thank you, Mr. Tulane. Glad to help. But the whole staff has a hand in healing. I'm leaving you here with Dr. Ransom.

TULANE. So long, Dr. Wyman. Again, I'm much obliged. *(CURTIS starts to leave, but remembering, turns back to RANDALL.)*

CURTIS. Don't forget, Randall: after clinic, we have Tumor Committee.

RANDALL. Thanks anyway, but I won't forget. I'm *chairing*, remember? *(CURTIS leaves, taking X-rays with him. RANDALL leads TULANE to the examining area and washes his hands at the sink before beginning the examination.)*

RANDALL. You're nearing the end of your treatment.

TULANE. Much obliged, Dr. Ransom, much obliged!

RANDALL. But how are things otherwise?

TULANE. Better than it *was.*

RANDALL. Better. But it could still be better yet?

TULANE. Still the same trouble as before ...

RANDALL. What trouble?

TULANE. Bills. After a bout with cancer, you expect that. But what gets me: I'm low income, all right, but the State won't pick up more of the balance.

RANDALL. That's why we hired Ms. Shepherd. Is *she* helping?

TULANE. Miss Vicky tapped her department funds for me. That helped.

RANDALL. But not enough, huh?

TULANE. Good of Miss Vicky to help. And she's aiming to get more for me.

RANDALL. Still, it's not enough!

TULANE. But—

RANDALL. You need a competent social-service person.

TULANE. Miss Vicky helps a lot, Dr. Ransom, and she's still working on it! Already got more food allowance. At least I don't go hungry, end of the month.

RANDALL. You need more than that!

TULANE. But—

RANDALL. More ought to be done!

TULANE. Like I told you, Dr. Ransom, Miss Vicky is sure workin' on it. *(Pause. TULANE looks thoughtful.)* Same as other things.

RANDALL. What other things?

TULANE. Like the way it was when I got sick. When you told me how bad it was, the way I felt inside. *(Pause.)* Miss Vicky knew it too.

RANDALL, *scoffing.* What would *she* know?

TULANE. Miss Vicky knew. Knew I wanted to die.

RANDALL. But you didn't. *I* saw to that!

TULANE. But it was Dr. Wyman too. And Miss Vicky. *Especially* Miss Vicky.

RANDALL. Your *doctors* cured you. Got that?

TULANE. But it was Miss Vicky too. She got me talkin' about things. Kind of talk I never had much use for.

RANDALL. How did she do it?

TULANE, *puzzled as to how to answer.* How she did it?

RANDALL. What did she tell you?

TULANE. What she told me? *(Pause.)*

RANDALL. Aha! You don't *know!*

TULANE. It was the way she *listened.*

RANDALL. *Listened?* The way she listened? Now look. If that woman's not doing her job, you tell me. Tell me, and I'll—

TULANE. I'm telling you, Dr. Ransom. Miss Vicky pulled me through.

RANDALL. There's some defect in services.

TULANE. But—

RANDALL. Let's move along. After clinic, I'm chairing Tumor Committee. *(He takes up his stethoscope and prepares to listen to TULANE's heart and lungs.)*

ACT ONE

SCENE 2

SETTING:

The conference room is arranged for a meeting. Podium is centered.

AT RISE:

AGNES DUDWORTH *enters and sits down. Immediately afterward VICTORIA rushes in.*

VICTORIA, *distraught and out of breath.* Ms. Dudworth! I looked for you all morning!

AGNES, *almost to herself.* I met with the board as well as the president.

VICTORIA. I thought I'd never find you.

AGNES. Something may be there for me ...

VICTORIA, *trying to be patient.* Yes, Ms. Dudworth.

AGNES. Time my ship dropped anchor! And that *Hazel Huff!*

VICTORIA. Yes, yes, of course. But—

AGNES. It may be ... *(Waking up.)* Oh, Ms. Shepherd! Obviously you wish to *say* something.

VICTORIA. Dr. Ransom! He—

AGNES. Dr. Ransom! Again? And I told him to *stop!*

VICTORIA. He— *(The steps and voices of others about to enter are heard. AGNES motions VICTORIA to be still. Immediately thereafter WINNIE and CURTIS enter from different directions. HAZEL HUFF then enters. She is about the same size and age as AGNES, though her demeanor is harsher. RANDALL enters last and goes to the podium.)*

RANDALL. Urgent matters are on our agenda. But first, an even more urgent matter about service to this great institution, and to our clients. *(Pause.)* Ms. Dudworth.

AGNES. Dr. Ransom.

RANDALL. Is your staff *effective*? *(Movements of chagrin by VICTORIA and CURTIS.)*

AGNES. What do you *mean*, Dr. Ransom?

RANDALL. Is *she (points to VICTORIA)* getting help?

AGNES. What are you *saying*?

RANDALL. There's reason to question the competence.

AGNES. Address Ms. Shepherd and me *privately*.

HAZEL. When staff fail to do their jobs, the entire committee is concerned!

AGNES. Ms. Shepherd *is* doing her job—a fine job.

CURTIS. Ms. Shepherd's great with our clients. And— *(RANDALL shushes CURTIS, keeps attention on AGNES.)*

RANDALL. Ms. Dudworth, some disagree with you.

AGNES. Then let them speak privately with Ms. Shepherd and me.

CURTIS. "Advice amidst a crowd is loathsome!"[2]

RANDALL. Everyone's complaining!

CURTIS, *disbelieving.* Complaining? About what?

WINNIE. About *everything.* Everything Victoria Shepherd ought to do, but won't do. *Everyone's* complaining.

RANDALL. Winnie's right. I'm a busy man. Yet my time's spent on complaints about Ms. Shepherd.

VICTORIA. *Who* is complaining? And about *what?*

RANDALL. Eh, well … it's … it's James Tulane. His health's better, but other matters are not well with him. I must speak bluntly. Mr. Tulane feels you are not serving him.

VICTORIA, *shocked.* Not serving him?

RANDALL. You should do more for him.

VICTORIA. I'm shocked.

RANDALL. You're unaware of your own faults.

VICTORIA. Precisely what are Mr. Tulane's complaints?

RANDALL, *self-righteous and indignant.* He's hungry because he can't buy food.

VICTORIA. Mr. Tulane *has* food, since we got help for him. *(Pause.)* But you know that, Dr. Ransom.

RANDALL, *feeling caught.* Well, he *does* need the State to pay more on his medical bills. You haven't done a *thing* about that!

VICTORIA. I told you this morning! I applied to a special fund for Mr. Tulane.

HAZEL. Now see here, young lady! Do your job! *(Agitated, she turns to VICTORIA and shakes her finger at her as she talks.)*

CURTIS. Watch it, Dr. Huff! "If your mouth turns into a knife, it'll cut off your lips!"[3]

AGNES. Hazel Huff, you know nothing about this!

VICTORIA. I applied to the State for Mr. Tulane. I supported his application with all that could succeed. But the State sets the standard. Other efforts are pending.

WINNIE. Big problem, Victoria Shepherd!

HAZEL, *before VICTORIA can answer WINNIE.* We need a *capable* staff, young lady! And a competent supervisor! *(Looks at AGNES.)*

AGNES. How would *you* know?

RANDALL. Obviously something's wrong. Otherwise, why all the complaints?

CURTIS. Ms. Shepherd's work is exemplary. She's of immense help to all. And she founded Healing Hands.

RANDALL. Forget Healing Hands! Clients are not getting what they need!

AGNES. The State determines the standard. It's the system.

RANDALL. This is the best system anywhere!

CURTIS. Says who?

RANDALL. Incompetence keeps help from the needy.

VICTORIA. We do everything possible.

RANDALL. Then why these complaints?

VICTORIA. It's something else. Something else is your real complaint.

WINNIE. What else could it be? It's a question of competence.

HAZEL, *to VICTORIA.* You can't do the job, so get out, and let a competent person in! *(AGNES motions HAZEL to be still.)*

CURTIS, *to HAZEL and WINNIE.* Look out, ladies! "Your tongue is your lion; let it loose and it will devour you!"[4]

RANDALL. *(Tries to shush CURTIS, replies relevant to what WINNIE and HAZEL said.)* Some agree with me.

AGNES. Address any complaints to Ms. Shepherd and me *alone*, and furthermore—

HAZEL. No! This concerns the entire committee.

AGNES, *losing her temper.* Hazel Huff, your concern is to get a chair you don't deserve!

HAZEL. Don't bandy words with me, Agnes Dudworth!

AGNES. You're a pain in the foot, Hazel Huff! Ms. Shepherd's work is beyond reproach!

RANDALL. Back to the central question: Is Ms. Shepherd competent to do the job she's hired for?

VICTORIA. I know what's bothering you, Dr. Ransom.

RANDALL, *angry, authoritative.* Respect the chair!

CURTIS. Speak as you wish, Ms. Shepherd!

RANDALL. Keep out of this, Wyman!

CURTIS. Something bothering you, Dr. Ransom? *(Pause.)* "A big head is a big load."[5]

RANDALL. Ms. Shepherd, I resent your insinuation!

AGNES. Let's move on.

CURTIS. But Ms. Shepherd said something's bothering Dr. Ransom. Let's hear it! *(Turns to RANDALL.)* What is it, Dr. Ransom?

RANDALL. Meeting adjourned!

VICTORIA. Dr. Ransom—

RANDALL. Meeting adjourned!

AGNES. There's the Healing Hands ceremony.

RANDALL. I said this meeting is adjourned!

CURTIS. But you wanted to talk about Ms. Shepherd's competence. So let's hear about Healing Hands! Then tell us what's gnawing you!

RANDALL. Everyone leave the room. Immediately. Meeting adjourned. (*Everyone files out of the meeting and off the stage except VICTORIA, RANDALL, AGNES, and HAZEL. Before leaving, CURTIS makes kind, supportive gestures toward VICTORIA, observed by RANDALL, who registers resentment. After the departure of CURTIS and WINNIE, VICTORIA and RANDALL stand in background in inaudible heated argument, RANDALL alternately acting apologetic and seeming recalcitrant. AGNES and HAZEL stand in the foreground; their exchange is audible.*)

AGNES. Hazel Huff, keep your feet out of matters that don't concern you!

HAZEL. At least they won't be in *your* shoes when *I* get promoted!

AGNES. You'll never get a foothold!

HAZEL. *Your* footsteps won't be heard!

AGNES. You won't even be a footnote!

HAZEL. *I* will take the chair! You and your little Ms. Shepherd'll get the boot!

AGNES. Keep your muddy soles off me and my staff!

HAZEL. But if the shoe fits—

AGNES. The shoe does *not* fit!

HAZEL. *(Laughs.)* Then you're a *tenderfoot!*

AGNES, *enraged.* You barmpot!

HAZEL. Lickspittle!

AGNES. Codswallop!

HAZEL. Dimbox! *(AGNES and HAZEL move closer to each other as the quarrel progresses. VICTORIA and RANDALL become aware that the two women are about to have a physical fight. They rush up and separate them.)*

VICTORIA. Ms. Dudworth!

RANDALL. Dr. Huff!

VICTORIA, *soothing.* Calm down, Ms. Dudworth. It's all right. *(Despite the efforts of VICTORIA and RANDALL, AGNES and HAZEL begin their shouting match again.)*

AGNES. You liripooping Scombroid!

HAZEL. You hagborn Groak!

AGNES. You sopping Scaramouch!

HAZEL. Toadeater!

AGNES. Fecaloid!

RANDALL. *(To HAZEL.)* Come, Dr. Huff. Doctors' lounge is free. Go in and compose yourself. *(He ushers HAZEL out of the room and off the stage but returns immediately.)*

AGNES, *looking in the direction of HAZEL.* Why that—! This is the last time I'll wear the motley for that bunion! I'll show her! If it's the last thing I do, I'll show her!

VICTORIA. Don't be upset, Ms. Dudworth. We'll get over. You and Dr. Huff, Dr. Ransom and me.

RANDALL. It's your work, Ms. Shepherd. Your work is *poor.*

AGNES. Poor? I never said that!

RANDALL. Dr. Huff agrees with me.

AGNES. That mudslinger! She's smearing my staff and me. You know that!

RANDALL. I know nothing.

AGNES. You, Dr. Ransom, are fully aware that Hazel Huff has her own motives for attacking my staff and me.

RANDALL. She only agrees that *some* of your staff are not up to the task!

VICTORIA, *to RANDALL.* What you *did* to me!

RANDALL. You're accusing me …

VICTORIA. You and I know what it is, don't we?

AGNES. What's going on? Clue me in!

VICTORIA. Dr. Ransom—

RANDALL, *flustered.* Uh, eh … it's all a … uh, misunderstanding. I mean—

VICTORIA. You're out for re—

RANDALL. Now, Ms. Shepherd, you know what a valuable employee I think you are. I was telling Dr. Burton—you know Dr. Burton, chief of the hospital? I told him what a jewel you are, and—

VICTORIA. Just moments ago you—

RANDALL. Really, Ms. Shepherd, I'm sure we can clear the misunderstanding. In fact, to start with, I apologize, and—

VICTORIA. I know what you're up to.

RANDALL. Let's make amends. I'm sorry. I apologize.

AGNES, *too eager to see the conflict smoothed over.* You didn't mean what you said about Ms. Shepherd?

RANDALL. I said something about Ms. Shepherd? All the same, I apologize. (*He looks puzzled. There is a movement of shock by VICTORIA.*)

VICTORIA. There's lots you owe an apology for!

RANDALL. I apologize. I'll never again do anything to hurt you.

VICTORIA. Ms. Dudworth ought to know.

RANDALL. Enough's been said!

VICTORIA. You grabbed my knee, and I ran from you!

RANDALL, *ignoring VICTORIA's new assertion.* I apologized.

AGNES, *also ignoring the new assertion.* You caused quite an upset in that meeting.

VICTORIA. Neither of you heard what I just said? *(To AGNES.)* Dr. Ransom grabbed my knee. And I had to run away from him! *(AGNES shows no awareness that VICTORIA has spoken.)*

RANDALL. Upset? I didn't mean to upset anyone.

AGNES. I was upset; and then Ms. Shepherd ...

RANDALL. I apologize to you both. I'm *really* very sorry.

AGNES. But why say those things?

RANDALL. A misunderstanding. It won't happen again. I apologize.

AGNES. All right, Dr. Ransom. Your apologies are accepted. I hope we all learn from this.

(This said, AGNES initiates vacating of the room. They all begin to gather up their things and move toward the door.)

RANDALL. Thank you, Ms. Dudworth. It's so good of you and Ms. Shepherd to accept my apology.

VICTORIA. I do not accept.

RANDALL. Please forgive me, Ms. Shepherd. Please. See the example of your superior! Please. I promise. It won't happen again.

VICTORIA. But you didn't own up—

RANDALL. Own up? To what?

VICTORIA. What you did!

RANDALL. I'm so sorry. You forgive me, don't you? *(The exchange continues as the three leave the scene, with the last few words being heard after they have left the stage. RANDALL returns immediately, followed by AGNES. During the following exchange between AGNES and RANDALL, VICTORIA can be seen in her office counseling CLIENTS.)*

AGNES. Again! Harassing Ms. Shepherd!

RANDALL. I'm sorry.

AGNES. But why?

RANDALL. You accepted my apology.

AGNES. For the meeting. But that knee-grabbing was before.

RANDALL. Nothing happened.

AGNES. What about the knee?

RANDALL. Knee? What knee?

AGNES. You know what I mean. She said—

RANDALL. You promised to let it go!

AGNES. I promised nothing! I told you: Ms. Shepherd is *not* to be dallied with.

RANDALL. Let *her* decide.

AGNES. Ms. Shepherd is a dedicated, hardworking young lady. Leave her alone so she can do her job.

RANDALL. If she insists.

AGNES. If she insists?

RANDALL. Right. I'll stop if she insists!

AGNES. Ms. Shepherd wants no part—

RANDALL. Others want it.

AGNES. But not Ms. Shepherd. She's not of the ilk.

RANDALL. You seem quite sure. *(Pause.)* But there's something I must ask of you.

AGNES. A favor? You're asking a favor?

RANDALL. A favor. *(Pause.)* The chair. Think you'll get it?

AGNES. I'll do anything to get it.

RANDALL. You want that chair. I see you want it.

AGNES. I've slaved for this institution. I've given of myself, down to the marrow. *(Pause.)* Yes. I want that chair.

RANDALL. Dr. Huff wants the same. The board favors her.

AGNES. But my years of loyal service should make *me* the choice.

RANDALL. Not if the board gets their way.

AGNES. I have board support.

RANDALL. But Dr. Huff has more. *(Pause.)* You *really* want the chair?

AGNES, *aghast*. Do I really want the chair?

RANDALL. Then help me with Ms. Shepherd.

AGNES. What do you mean?

RANDALL. Ms. Shepherd must belong to me.

AGNES. What?

RANDALL. She must come to me. *(Pause.)* Or she can't *be* here.

AGNES. I don't understand.

RANDALL. She must be mine.

AGNES. What have I to do with *that*?

RANDALL. Victoria Shepherd's mine—or she can't be here!

AGNES. You are not the one to decide that.

RANDALL. Are you aware that my father-in-law plays chess with the president of this institution?

AGNES. No.

RANDALL. But you must know the president has the final word as to the chair.

AGNES. What would you expect of Ms. Shepherd?

RANDALL. To be amenable.

AGNES, *dismissive*. You expect her to join the flirtgigs, the flouncies, the—

RANDALL. Give me your word.

AGNES. To do what?

RANDALL. To agree with me if she fails to ... uh, measure up.

AGNES, *scornful*. What if I *don't* agree?

RANDALL, *cold and hard*. The chair, Ms. Dudworth. The chair! Without *me*, what will happen?

AGNES. It's so cut and dried.

RANDALL. (*He handles a few dried flowers from a shelf, may even sniff them.*) As cut and dried as these flowers for Ms. Shepherd's Healing Hands.

AGNES. You staked out your claim.

RANDALL. Let's join our stakes. For your garden. Soil that sticks together is always stronger.

AGNES. Then, with the president, you'll say a word for me?

RANDALL. Ms. Shepherd. She must be mine.

AGNES. I told you: she's not like the others.

RANDALL, *sneering*. A woman of the vanquished!

AGNES. *Vanquished*? Because she's—

RANDALL. You don't agree with my ideology.

AGNES. Ideology! Don't plant that. It won't grow!

RANDALL. The roots are there.

AGNES. The seeds are rancid.

RANDALL. The roots—

AGNES. *Make-believe! (Pause.)* The roots are make-believe!

RANDALL. *Make-believe!* You say make-believe? *(Pause.)* Once upon a time I was six years old, and my playmate was five. *(Pause.)* I see her now. My playmate's hair is knotted wool. Her skin is like coal dust. *(Pause.)* And the sun rises and sets on her smile. She laughs, and the playground is a gazing ball where I cavort with a fairy princess, astride a unicorn. *(Pause.)*

AGNES. That's the kind of make-believe—

RANDALL, *stopping her with a sign.* One day my father sees us. *(Pause.)* Me with my fairy princess. He calls me to him. "Don't ever let me catch you playing with a black kid again, you understand?" Sparks rage from his eyes. I tremble. My uncle is there. He says to my dad, "When he gets grown, he'll see what that kind's good for!" A red smirk. I look at my dad. The raging sparks become a lurid wink. He and my uncle are wrapped in a haze. A strange haze. And I am outside it, alone. All alone outside the haze.

AGNES. Throw off that memory! All that happened when you were six years old! Gazing balls, fairy princesses, unicorns, raging sparks, lurid winks, red smirks! Put them on my ship, raise the anchor, and she floats them away. Look! My ship is sailing them away, *away!*

RANDALL. The gazing ball goes blank. Fairy princess? Unicorn? All swept away by the haze. And I am outside it. *Alone.*

AGNES. Ship's away with that memory. Look! She's out to sea. She dumps that refuse into the deep. And she returns with a throne: a golden chair, for me.

RANDALL. Your ship is taking on water! Possess the vanquished!

AGNES, *scoffing mockingly.* "The vanquished!"

RANDALL. The vanquished! She comes to me, or she's through! *(Pause.) If* you want the chair.

AGNES. You'll *see* that I get it?

RANDALL. She's *mine,* or she goes.

AGNES. What am I to do?

RANDALL. Tell Ms. Shepherd I am not satisfied. She must *please* me.

AGNES. And then?

RANDALL. If this fails, Ms. Shepherd goes!

AGNES. Agreed! I'll talk with her right away.

(END of ACT I)

ACT TWO

SETTING:

Early afternoon. Conference room.

AT RISE:

VICTORIA is seated, writing in charts. CURTIS enters. They exchange looks briefly without speaking.

CURTIS. "Silence is also a form of speech."[6]

VICTORIA. Everything's all right.

CURTIS. How can you concentrate in this whirlwind?

VICTORIA. As usual.

CURTIS. "The plant bows before the wind. But she only bows to rise up again."[7]

VICTORIA. Believe me, I'm okay.

CURTIS. The wind rages.

VICTORIA. I breathed my life into these walls.

43

CURTIS. Commendable.

VICTORIA, *warmly grateful.* You stood by me.

CURTIS. Since when has commendable work ever assured anyone of a job?

VICTORIA. Ms. Dudworth understands.

CURTIS. Understands in *your* way or in some other way?

VICTORIA. Oh, him! Since Ms. Dudworth knows, why worry?

CURTIS. I spoke with Ransom about that knee business.

VICTORIA. You spoke with him!

CURTIS. He denies everything. Says others will believe him, not you.

VICTORIA. Of course he denies!

CURTIS. File a complaint!

VICTORIA. I told Ms. Dudworth.

CURTIS. What's she doing?

VICTORIA. She couldn't say anything. *He* was there.

CURTIS. "When the music changes so should the dance!"[8]

VICTORIA. Ms. Dudworth's got a grip on it.

CURTIS. How firm?

VICTORIA, *exasperated*. Please, Dr. Wyman!

CURTIS. "Eggs have no business dancing with stones."[9]

VICTORIA. But Ms. Dudworth *understands*. She appreciates all my work: for Healing Hands, for our clients, for—

CURTIS. Know the tale of the pheasant and the python?

VICTORIA. A pheasant flies, and a python crawls. But, no, I *don't* know the tale of the pheasant and the python, and I won't hear it. Your stories—

CURTIS. The python was surrounded by fire. Having no escape, when he saw a pheasant flying over, he said, "Take me on your back and fly me away from this fire." So the pheasant took the python on his back and flew him to a safe place. Arriving at safety, the pheasant said to the python, "Continue on your journey," but the python said, "I am hungry. I shall eat you."[10]

VICTORIA. But Ms. Dudworth wouldn't do that. She's a pearl!

CURTIS. A pearl as in the oyster?

VICTORIA. Yes. A real pearl!

CURTIS. Or like the faux pearls bought and sold everywhere? (*He indicates the faux pearls collected for Healing Hands Center.*)

VICTORIA. Ms. Dudworth is genuine!

CURTIS, *patiently*. Ms. Shepherd, since you and I are both of the Black race, there's something I must say.

VICTORIA. Let's remember there's just one race: the human race!

CURTIS. Is that *all* to remember?

VICTORIA. What else *could* there be? My parents always taught me: in the many there's only one—one glorious race of human beings!

CURTIS. Now you listen to me: "A new broom sweeps clean. But an old broom knows the corners!"[11] *(He dramatizes his point by using the broom that WINNIE left in the conference room.)*

VICTORIA. No disrespect, Dr. Wyman, but this new broom knows a few corners! We have a new age. A new century. Let's have new thinking about race. Let's not think of ourselves as Black. Let's think of ourselves as belonging to the one great human race! Never forget that!

CURTIS. There *is* something I won't forget. *(Pause.)* I once had my own cancer-research project.

VICTORIA. Ms. Dudworth says you were in high esteem. You were the only one doing that research.

CURTIS. My own cancer-research project. Did the work on my own time, shared the findings. Published the results.

VICTORIA. Something wonderful was happening.

CURTIS. Because of that *work*—*my* work—this hospital was awarded money for cancer research.

VICTORIA. Oh, the hospital should be very proud of you, Dr. Wyman!

CURTIS. Naturally, since the grant was awarded on *my* research, I thought I'd be the one to head the new program.

VICTORIA. Naturally.

CURTIS. But I was not selected.

VICTORIA. Not selected?

CURTIS. Someone else was chosen to head the research. Someone else to use the monies awarded for *my* work. *(Pause.)*

VICTORIA. Horrible!

CURTIS. Until then I always thought of myself as strong.

VICTORIA. It was painful for you, Dr. Wyman.

CURTIS. *That's* the what. Now you say the *why*.

VICTORIA. But something should have been done!

CURTIS. I exhausted the avenues for redress. Moved on.

VICTORIA. But that was long ago. It's different now.

CURTIS. *How* different?

VICTORIA. Different! Now we can be just one big human race!

CURTIS. When the race is won … *(Pause.)* Understand the systemic—

VICTORIA. The what?

CURTIS. Systemic. Satan in the cells. Growing wild, profligate, degenerate. The surgeon removes one monstrosity, but others lurk. Vessels spew to nurse the wretched progeny, invading, appropriating. A cancer in the system!

VICTORIA. What's to be done?

CURTIS. What ought *you* to do? *(Pause. VICTORIA is uncertain how to reply.)*

VICTORIA. *You* have the proverbs.

CURTIS. The proverbs are the light on my scalpel probing my way through errant cells.

VICTORIA. So? The African proverbs. Then what?

CURTIS. In my treatise, the proverbs are the medicine, spurring the victim to heal.

VICTORIA. I'd like to see your treatise.

CURTIS. First page is ready. I'll give you a copy.

VICTORIA. Please do. Not that I need inspiration.

CURTIS. Beware the cells that multiply. It happened to me.

VICTORIA. You were passed over.

CURTIS. There's an army of metastases! But do not succumb.

VICTORIA. What's the antidote?

CURTIS. "What comes when you already know of it robs you of far less than if you were unaware."[12] *(Pause.)*

VICTORIA. What to do?

CURTIS. File charges. Do it now.

VICTORIA. Too hasty!

CURTIS. File immediately. And write down everything—*everything*—anyone says to you.

VICTORIA. But I don't see …

CURTIS. Keep an account. For instance, this conversation with me: make a note of it, to recall the admonition.

VICTORIA. And I should keep notes on talks with Dr. Ransom and Ms. Dudworth?

CURTIS. Especially for them, and for all others.

VICTORIA. Really, Dr. Wyman! *(She laughs at his caution.)* You won't believe this, but—

CURTIS. Believe what?

VICTORIA. He *apologized*.

CURTIS. Ransom?

VICTORIA. None other than Dr. Ransom.

CURTIS, *ironical.* Apologized, huh?

VICTORIA. He's sorry for the meeting. Soon he'll apologize for what else he did.

CURTIS. "There can be no bargain between the spider and the fly."[13] *(Pause.)* Listen! *(Just then AGNES enters carrying a load of charts that she puts on the table.)*

AGNES. I'm interrupting?

CURTIS. Not at all, Ms. Dudworth. I'm just leaving.

AGNES. Don't rush. Finish what you were about.

CURTIS. Briefing Ms. Shepherd on the ... uh ... inner workings of our great institution. You and I have seen a lot, haven't we?

AGNES. *(Preoccupied with her writing, she does not look up.)* Here it's no different from any other.

CURTIS, *conceding ironically.* You're right. *(Pause.)* Good-bye for now.

VICTORIA. So long, Dr. Wyman.

AGNES. Good-bye. *(CURTIS exits.)*

AGNES. A conference, Ms. Shepherd.

VICTORIA. Yes, Ms. Dudworth.

AGNES. For my star to rise, my deck must be polished, my crew alert.

VICTORIA. All right, Ms. Dudworth.

AGNES. No unswept corners to darken the glow of my beacon. My light shining in the ship garden. Preparedness!

VICTORIA. Yes, Ms. Dudworth.

AGNES. The topic of our conference ...

VICTORIA. I'm ready.

AGNES. Ms. Shepherd, you and I talked since that, uh, *upset* with Dr. Ransom this morning.

VICTORIA. Yes.

AGNES. And then I talked with Dr. Ransom. And I must tell you: Dr. Ransom wants very much to get along with you.

VICTORIA. After what he did!

AGNES. Dr. Ransom does not wish to upset you.

VICTORIA. But you *know* what happened!

AGNES. But then I talked with Dr. Ransom. *(Pause.)* He was amused. He truly likes you, Ms. Shepherd. You can be his friend.

VICTORIA. His friend!

AGNES. It's understandable. Dr. Ransom is a handsome man. You're not the first young lady who dreamt he took a fancy to her—

VICTORIA. *Dreamt!*

AGNES. Even so, my dear, it might be a good thing. Dr. Ransom may be fully amenable.

VICTORIA. *What?*

AGNES. A handsome doctor. Chief of his discipline. It isn't surprising that you would be attracted to him, and—

VICTORIA, *angry.* But—

AGNES. And it's easier to believe he's taken a fancy to *you* than vice versa!

VICTORIA, *flustered.* Dr. Ransom has a wife!

AGNES, *more to herself than to VICTORIA.* And a father-in-law who plays chess with the hospital president!

VICTORIA, *confused about the turn of the conversation.* What could that have to do with me?

AGNES. Doubtless that chess game interests *me* more than you. *(More to herself than VICTORIA.)* And a pawn can be a ladder.

VICTORIA. What do you mean?

AGNES. Nothing. *(Pause.)* I want to end this talk.

VICTORIA. Yes, Ms. Dudworth.

AGNES. Let me say this: Ms. Shepherd, Dr. Ransom is too important a man for you to fail to get along with.

VICTORIA. But I—

AGNES. Dr. Ransom spoke about your work.

VICTORIA. What are his concerns?

AGNES. Just a general feeling about, uh … your inadequacy.

VICTORIA. *What* inadequacy?

AGNES. He wants to be close with you. He believes the two of you could work closely, to the benefit of all. *(Pause.)* You know what I mean?

VICTORIA. No. I don't know what you mean. And since Dr. Ransom won't specify his complaints, then how do I know what *he* means?

AGNES. Why specify every detail? Sometimes one can simply say what one wants.

VICTORIA. And what does Dr. Ransom want?

AGNES. You, Ms. Shepherd. Dr. Ransom wants *you*.

VICTORIA. Ridiculous! How *could* he want me?

AGNES. I am apprising you of his expectations.

VICTORIA. Dr. Ransom has no authority over me.

AGNES. He *is* Chief of Tumor Service.

VICTORIA. That doesn't make him correct in his judgment! Nor does it give him power over me!

AGNES. He says what he wants!

VICTORIA. You've *never* been this way.

AGNES. Learn to get along. *(Pause.)* And *I* must focus on my career!

VICTORIA. But—

AGNES. Enough!

VICTORIA. Hear me out!

AGNES. I have heard you, Ms. Shepherd. Now what I say is this: you'd *better* improve. You must learn to get along.

VICTORIA. But how can I get along with that man?

AGNES. Dr. Ransom likes you.

VICTORIA. He *grabbed* me!

AGNES. He really likes you, Ms. Shepherd. He wants to be your friend.

VICTORIA. What do you mean, "*likes*" me?

AGNES. He *really* likes you. *(Pause.)* Why not try ...

VICTORIA. Try what? *(Pause.)*

AGNES. Something extra ...

VICTORIA. Ms. Dudworth. You once knew me.

AGNES. Either you want this job, or—

VICTORIA. I don't understand!

AGNES. You *must* improve.

VICTORIA. But we talked about Dr. Ransom's attitude. You even *spoke* with him.

AGNES. Now I've had a real *talk* with him, I understand better.

VICTORIA. This change! *(RANDALL and WINNIE arrive to eavesdrop just outside the door.)*

AGNES. Your work will be monitored in every detail.

VICTORIA. But—

AGNES. Show me your work, everything!

54

VICTORIA. But—

AGNES. Now come with me. To my office, and then … (*AGNES exits the scene, with VICTORIA following, AGNES's last words being heard after the two have left the stage. WINNIE and RANDALL enter as soon as AGNES and VICTORIA have left the room. VICTORIA follows AGNES to AGNES's office, where, during the RANDALL/WINNIE audible dialogue, AGNES is observed inaudibly yelling at VICTORIA.*)

RANDALL. How d'ya like that: "Your work will be monitored in every detail!" Now that's telling her!

WINNIE. Oh Randy, just think: we'll soon be rid of that little twerp!

RANDALL. No cakewalk through the jungle!

WINNIE. But how did you manage Agnes Dudworth?

RANDALL. Old huggy bear knows how!

WINNIE, *hugging him.* That's my Randy Dandy!

RANDALL. And that's not all. You and I have some, uh, *paperwork.* (*Laughs and winks maliciously.*)

WINNIE, *understanding, turns her attention to the charts.* The charts.

RANDALL. (Nods.) The thing is … what we gotta do is … (*Motions as if removing documents from charts.*)

WINNIE. (*Removes some service sheets from several charts and holds them up.*) Like these?

RANDALL. Yeah, those are the ones she—

WINNIE. So it's these ...

RANDALL. *(Picks up service sheet.)* Listen to what she wrote: *(Reads.)* "Mr. Tulane is cheerful since his therapy and the counselor-supported efforts to increase his income. All this together with remission of his cancer ..." etc, etc, etc.

WINNIE. She wrote that, huh? Why that, that little ... oh!

RANDALL. Now don't worry your pretty head, my Winnie buttercup. We'll take care of this!

WINNIE. We take out the new ones *and* the old ones?

RANDALL. I think, well, if we take out the old ones, those might already have been seen.

WINNIE. Okay, the new ones. Just the new ones. Start now?

RANDALL. No, not yet.

WINNIE. Not yet?

RANDALL. Later I'll give the word as to when—and *if.*

WINNIE. Oh, huggy buggy! Let's start right now! Oh, I can't wait to show that, that ...

RANDALL. Bit by bit we'll show the little darkling! A signal when it's time! Wait for my signal! *(RANDALL and WINNIE laugh in the manner of persons sharing a mischievous secret. CURTIS, unaware of RANDALL and WINNIE's treachery, enters. He beckons RANDALL, then calls AGNES, indicating the need for the three of them to confer. CURTIS leads them to his office, which adjoins an edge of the conference room and is on the opposite side of the stage from the examining room.*

VICTORIA has left AGNES's office and returned to her own. There she briefly holds her face in her hands, in dejection. But she rallies and calls a waiting CLIENT into her office. WINNIE remains seated at the conference table, working with charts. Lights go down on her.)

CURTIS, *to AGNES, with irritation.* You yelled at Ms. Shepherd!

AGNES. It's *my* job to see that the staff does *theirs.*

CURTIS. By howling like that?

AGNES. Ms. Shepherd is difficult.

CURTIS. "Can you wear two faces under one hat?"[14]

RANDALL. You're bundling up with Ms. Shepherd? That won't wash it out!

CURTIS. Why you—

AGNES. Dr. Ransom enlightened me about Ms. Shepherd.

CURTIS. What did Ransom promise you?

AGNES. *Promise* me? Are you accusing me of ...? *(CURTIS nods.)* I'd never—

CURTIS. You're bailing out?

AGNES. My loyalty has served this ship. This is my chance to rise. Why let Ms. Shepherd bar my way?

RANDALL, *to CURTIS.* Gold for a trifle?

CURTIS, *to AGNES*. Ms. Shepherd founded Healing Hands. Think of the clients. Mr. Tulane!

AGNES. Dr. Ransom complained. He—

CURTIS. "The vulture you name taboo: Why eat his eggs?"[15]

AGNES. Ms. Shepherd can help me if she becomes a bit more … *(Gropes for words.)*

RANDALL. Cooperative! More teamwork!

CURTIS. Of all the—

AGNES. I gave my life to these walls, these floors, these shelves. Why let Ms. Shepherd block my elevation? Never! I must reap the harvest that my best years have sown.

CURTIS. To fertilize your soil, you bury the hopes of this young woman.

RANDALL. Keep out of this, Wyman!

CURTIS. Human sacrifice!

AGNES. *(Looks at her watch.)* Gotta go! I'm late for my meeting! I'll teach that Hazel Huff! I'll show her! That foot fetish! *(She rushes off. CURTIS and RANDALL stand glowering at each other. Lights go down on CURTIS and RANDALL. Lights come up on AGNES conferring with 1st EMPLOYEE and 2nd EMPLOYEE in her office. They may be portrayed by any two of the same actors portraying MR. TULANE, MRS. SIMMONS, or DR. HAZEL HUFF. Both of the TWO EMPLOYEES may be in drag.)*

1st EMPLOYEE. *(Hands records to AGNES.)* The records on Dr. Huff.

AGNES. Is this all?

2nd EMPLOYEE. All from the archives.

1st EMPLOYEE. We searched as you ordered.

AGNES. Now listen, you two!

1st EMPLOYEE and 2nd EMPLOYEE, *replying in unison.* Yes, Ms. Dudworth.

AGNES. Not a word to anyone! Your solemn promise not to breathe a word.

1st EMPLOYEE. You have my promise, Ms. Dudworth.

2nd EMPLOYEE. Not a word to anyone.

AGNES, *looking at documents handed to her earlier.* A patient was injured in an accident caused by Dr. Huff. What happened?

1st EMPLOYEE. Dr. Huff spilled a chemical on a patient, resulting in cancer, deterioration, and—

AGNES, *eagerly.* Death?

2nd EMPLOYEE. Well, no. According to records, the patient survived, but barely by the hairs of her eyebrows.

1st EMPLOYEE. And died *later* …

2nd EMPLOYEE. Of *unrelated* causes.

1st EMPLOYEE. Right. The patient died later of causes unrelated to Dr. Huff's carelessness.

AGNES. Be that as it may. My report will say the patient died of Dr. Huff's incompetence.

1st EMPLOYEE. But it says here the patient *recovered* from Dr. Huff's bungling, but then died of unrelated causes.

AGNES. Causes are never unrelated. Give me those records. I'll see that the causes are, uh ... *properly* related.

2nd EMPLOYEE. Ms. Dudworth, you *prove* it by your brilliance!

1st EMPLOYEE. Ms. Dudworth, you will prevail!

AGNES. The two of you will be richly rewarded—once I get that chair! *(Lights go down on AGNES, 1st EMPLOYEE, and 2nd EMPLOYEE. Lights come up on VICTORIA and RANDALL in the examining room space used as RANDALL's office. VICTORIA lingers warily in the doorway.)*

VICTORIA. You called me?

RANDALL. Come in. Don't be afraid. I won't hurt you.

VICTORIA. Trust *you?*

RANDALL. I am truly sorry. I apologize for everything!

VICTORIA. But—

RANDALL. I was wrong. Dear Victoria, please, please accept my humble apologies.

VICTORIA. I can't.

RANDALL. Forgive me.

VICTORIA, *agitated. But you did this!*

RANDALL. Did what, my love?

VICTORIA, *seething.* Your *what?* Why, you ... you ...

RANDALL. Go ahead, darling. What names do you call me? I accept them all.

VICTORIA. How could you do this? Ms. Dudworth is watching my every move!

RANDALL. She'll see you in better light.

VICTORIA. You turned her against me!

RANDALL. I spoke in your favor.

VICTORIA. You put me in *dis*favor!

RANDALL. I spoke a mountain of praises for you. *(VICTORIA is aghast.)* Give me your hands. Let them heal me.

VICTORIA. They'd rather do otherwise. *(Indicates that she feels like strangling him.)*

RANDALL. I submit as their victim if only to feel their touch.

VICTORIA. Hurting precedes healing.

RANDALL. The wound will heal my heart.

VICTORIA. I'll speak with Ms. Dudworth. I'll make her understand!

RANDALL. Know what's needed?

VICTORIA. *You* wouldn't know!

RANDALL. Smile. Just smile.

VICTORIA. Let me do my work. Everyone's excited about the Center: the sad, the ill, the isolated. They feel that life is more worthwhile. Clients are *waiting* for Healing Hands.

RANDALL. Your hands have been at work. Give them a rest, to do *different* work.

VICTORIA. My work is enough.

RANDALL. Dear, dear Victoria, I'm an easy guy. *(Pause.)* Just smile a little ... smile ...

(He slowly moves toward her.)

VICTORIA, *slowly backing away from RANDALL.* You *frowned* on me to Ms. Dudworth!

RANDALL, *soothingly.* My brow never wrinkled.

VICTORIA. You spoke ill of me.

RANDALL. I spoke flowers of you, only mine were in fresh bloom.

VICTORIA. I'll make Ms. Dudworth understand!

RANDALL. Ms. Dudworth hopes to increase her rank on the ship. Her loyalty may increase her blooming in the ship garden.

VICTORIA. I'm loyal too.

RANDALL. Agnes Dudworth has plowed and planted.

VICTORIA. My seeds are in the ground. Some have even sprouted.

RANDALL. Agnes Dudworth and Hazel Huff want the same harvest.

VICTORIA. Let them pit spades and hoes—

RANDALL. It'll be a fight! *(Pause.)* Except ... Ms. Dudworth and I have, uh, you might say, ties to the same people.

VICTORIA. Ms. Dudworth is hopeful.

RANDALL. May be more than a hope. More a matter of ... her ship! But back to you. You want your job.

VICTORIA. Yes.

RANDALL. There's reason you should keep it.

VICTORIA. Then let me! Let me!

RANDALL. Listen to what I told you: smile, smile, and smile. *(He slowly moves toward her.)*

VICTORIA. You don't understand ...

RANDALL. You're a pretty woman when you smile. Prettier still if the smile's for me.

VICTORIA. But ... but ...

RANDALL. *(Gently caresses VICTORIA's hair, speaking softly, pliantly.)* Victoria, *dear* Victoria. *(Pause.)* I'm an *easy* guy. It's your choice. All yours. *(She shrinks back from RANDALL.)*

VICTORIA. What?

RANDALL. Your choice. All yours. (*RANDALL and VICTORIA stand facing each other, motionless. VICTORIA suddenly gasps and rushes out. Lights go up on WINNIE in the conference room, with charts. RANDALL quickly makes a sign to her, and she begins removing service sheets from the charts. Lights go down on RANDALL and WINNIE. Lights come up on VICTORIA rushing into corridor, where she meets MRS. SIMMONS.*)

VICTORIA. Mrs. Simmons!

MRS. SIMMONS. (*She keeps going.*) In a hurry, honey!

VICTORIA. I left you messages.

MRS. SIMMONS. Been real busy, child! (*She continues to move along.*)

VICTORIA. But wait—

MRS. SIMMONS. Can't stop!

VICTORIA. You're in such a hurry!

MRS. SIMMONS. When it's trouble, I'm off!

VICTORIA. So you *have* heard about me!

MRS. SIMMONS. And trouble is catching!

VICTORIA. But wait—

MRS. SIMMONS. Trouble is the most contagious disease alive!

VICTORIA. But— (*MRS. SIMMONS rushes off. VICTORIA sighs, enters office of AGNES in response to AGNES's motioning her to come for a conference.*)

VICTORIA. Ms. Dudworth?

AGNES, *almost hysterical, indicating charts.* What's the meaning of this?

VICTORIA. Something's wrong?

AGNES. You ought to know!

VICTORIA. But I don't.

AGNES. How could you be so unaware of what you're doing—or *not* doing!

VICTORIA. What?

AGNES, *irritable, even frantic. Where* are the service sheets?

VICTORIA. Service sheets? They're where they always are: in the charts.

AGNES. They are not!

VICTORIA. Not in the charts?

AGNES. None are in the charts.

VICTORIA. You overlooked them. Where I put them: just between the—

AGNES. I *know* where they're *supposed* to be. They are not there!

VICTORIA. I can't believe it!

AGNES. *(Hands VICTORIA a few charts.)* See for yourself!

VICTORIA. *(Flips through charts, becoming progressively more frantic as she continuously fails to find the service sheets.)* I ... I don't understand ...

AGNES, *vehemently.* The hospital requires, *requires* timely documentation!

VICTORIA. I know, I know, but—

AGNES, *ignoring her.* You must, absolutely *must* place a service sheet in each chart.

VICTORIA. But that's what I always do. I place them in the charts!

AGNES. I want the truth, Ms. Shepherd!

VICTORIA. Ms. Dudworth, I put them there. I did!

AGNES. I am gravely concerned.

VICTORIA, *bewildered. I ... I ...*

AGNES. Where are the documents? *(Pause.)* You haven't done them? You haven't done the work?

VICTORIA. Someone ... someone must have removed—

AGNES. There's no excuse for this!

VICTORIA. But someone must have *removed* the service sheets. *(Pause.)*

AGNES. What? You're suggesting someone removed the sheets after you placed them in the charts?

VICTORIA. Yes. Someone must have—

AGNES. Impossible! That never happens!

VICTORIA. But it *did* happen. The service sheets were *removed!*

AGNES. How do you know?

VICTORIA. I *put* them there. *(Pause.)*

AGNES. Ms. Shepherd.

VICTORIA. Yes, Ms. Dudworth.

AGNES. Dr. Ransom and I, well …

VICTORIA. Yes?

AGNES. Dr. Ransom and I think you would be happier elsewhere.

VICTORIA. What do you mean?

AGNES. Dr. Ransom feels you're not doing well here.

VICTORIA. There's some mistake.

AGNES. No. Dr. Ransom and I believe you should move on.

VICTORIA. This morning you disagreed with Dr. Ransom.

AGNES. I *did?*

VICTORIA. You disagreed with him. You disagreed with everything he said.

AGNES. Now I see what's at stake!

VICTORIA. What?

AGNES. It's the stakes!

VICTORIA. *What* did you say?

AGNES, *coming to herself.* Nothing!

VICTORIA. You said "it's the stakes"!

AGNES. We'll all be burned at the stake if we don't revise these records!

VICTORIA. No. You said "it's the stakes." You're thinking of the stakes!

AGNES. Ms. Shepherd! I have no reason to say such a thing. *(Pause.)* But that aside, I want to talk about you. Dr. Ransom is asking that you resign.

VICTORIA. *Resign?*

AGNES. It's generous of Dr. Ransom: to allow you to resign, to leave your position voluntarily to maintain your dignity, as you quietly vacate—

VICTORIA, *enraged.* I won't go along with this, this—

AGNES. What will happen?

VICTORIA. I'll fight!

AGNES. You're naive.

VICTORIA. I won't resign. I refuse!

AGNES. Accept the generosity.

VICTORIA. Generosity? I—

AGNES. Resign, Ms. Shepherd. Dr. Ransom and I are in full agreement. Give me your written resignation.

VICTORIA. I ... I'll fight!

AGNES, *scornful*. Fight? Fight with what?

VICTORIA. With all my might!

AGNES. Resign, Ms. Shepherd. Dr. Ransom and I are backed by this entire institution.

VICTORIA. But it's *wrong!*

AGNES. And stop vying for sympathy. I have no use for that! *(Pause. More to herself than to VICTORIA.)* Not when there might be a prize for me. My years of loyalty paid with a glorious chair where I am supreme.

VICTORIA. I, I'll complain. I—

AGNES. Resign, Ms. Shepherd. The institution is for Dr. Ransom and me.

VICTORIA. Please, so much is pending: the clients, Mr. Tulane, Healing Hands! Please, Ms. Dudworth. *(Pause.)* Credit for my work goes to you as well as to me.

AGNES. Give me your resignation immediately—in writing. Once it's in my hands, I'll give you a good job reference.

VICTORIA. I don't want a job reference.

AGNES. It'll help in finding a new job.

VICTORIA. But I *have* a job. Let me stay.

AGNES. I expect your resignation, in *writing,* before the end of the day.

VICTORIA. But—

AGNES. That will be all, Ms. Shepherd. *(AGNES stands and indicates the door. VICTORIA rises and leaves dejectedly. Lights go down on AGNES. VICTORIA goes to her office where lights go up. She sits at the table, briefly holds her head in her hands, then starts to write. Finishing, she reads aloud what she has just written.)*

VICTORIA, *reading.* To Ms. Agnes Dudworth: As you requested, I hereby submit my resignation, effective immediately. *(Pause.)* Sincerely, Victoria Shepherd. *(She reads as if the matter is fully decided. She is resigning. She then becomes distraught and sits holding her head in her hands. CURTIS enters. She looks up.)*

CURTIS. *(He is momentarily startled by her look of sadness.)* "For news of the heart, ask the face."[16]

VICTORIA. I'm resigning, Dr. Wyman!

CURTIS. No!

VICTORIA. Listen. *(Reads.)* To Ms. Agnes Dudworth: As you requested, I hereby submit my resignation, effective immediately. Sincerely, Victoria Shepherd.

CURTIS. What's going *on?*

VICTORIA. Ms. Dudworth and Dr. Ransom. They want me to resign.

CURTIS. But why?

VICTORIA. The service sheets I put in the charts?

CURTIS. Sure, the ones from this morning?

VICTORIA. Yes, those. *(Pause.)* I put them in, but they were removed!

CURTIS, *nodding suspiciously.* Removed, huh?

VICTORIA. And now Ms. Dudworth won't believe me. She thinks they were never there!

CURTIS. What happened to those documents?

VICTORIA. Someone removed them. But what's the use? Ms. Dudworth won't believe me!

CURTIS. So you're *resigning?*

VICTORIA. The entire institution backs Ms. Dudworth and Dr. Ransom.

CURTIS. Some feel differently.

VICTORIA. The chiefs back Dr. Ransom and Ms. Dudworth.

CURTIS. Don't resign, Ms. Shepherd. You're doing wonderful work. Lead us at Healing Hands. We're depending on you. And we will *help* you.

VICTORIA. There's nothing anyone can do. And nothing I can do.

CURTIS. "The bird that refuses to fly goes to sleep hungry."[17]

VICTORIA. This bird can only sit on the tree.

CURTIS. "Stones are thrown at the bird that sits on the tree."[18]

VICTORIA. But my wings are held hostage.

CURTIS. Fight and press on to the end.

VICTORIA. The walls are too high.

CURTIS. "Fight and press to the end, only then may you be victorious."[19]

VICTORIA. They'll force me out!

CURTIS. Don't leave, Ms. Shepherd. Don't leave.

VICTORIA. But there's nothing else for me. *Nothing.* I must resign.

CURTIS. Are you so timid?

VICTORIA. Now look here, Dr. Wyman: no one has ever called me timid. I can stand up to anyone, anything.

CURTIS. Ms. Shepherd—

VICTORIA. But if I let them force me—

CURTIS. You don't have to.

VICTORIA. And with that on my record—

CURTIS. Ms. Shepherd, I must be on my way. I only stopped to give you a message.

VICTORIA. A message?

CURTIS. Mr. Tulane needs to see you. Be here any moment.

VICTORIA. Not now. This isn't the time.

CURTIS. It's about a letter.

VICTORIA. But—

CURTIS. He'll be here any minute. *(CURTIS starts to leave, but remembers he wants to give VICTORIA a copy of the first page of his treatise. It is printed on gold paper.)* Oh, I promised you a copy of my treatise. Here's the first page. Take a look. *(CURTIS places his paper on the table and starts to leave again, but comes back.)* Now remember, Mr. Tulane needs to see you. *Wait* for him. *(CURTIS leaves.)*

VICTORIA. *(Walks to where CURTIS left his paper, picks it up, and reads. But the voice heard saying the words of the proverbs is that of CURTIS himself.)*

Though venom spawns from cell to cell,
Berserks the blood with rank decay,
Slinging tentacles that expel,
And devour every vital ray—

Bow not beneath the burning onslaught;
Torrential tears oil the attack;
Recall the courage you were taught;
Facing the storm, you don't look back.

Victim weeps, enemy reaps![20]

Bathe your cells in wisdom's light;
Warm your heart in the fire of their glow;

Do not shrink from the fight.

Let strength and courage flow.
Wisdom in the heart is like light in a jug.[21]

Arm your fingers with the scalpel;
Dissect the flesh you must amend;
Render the cells whole and well;
Be confident and do not bend.

Stitch fortitude into each fiber,
Treat the wound and be the healer!

Endurance pierces marble.[22]

(Moved, VICTORIA puts down the treatise. She takes up her letter of resignation and reads it again. This time her voice is entirely perfunctory, utterly lacking conviction.)

To Ms. Dudworth: I hereby submit my resignation, effective immediately. Sincerely, Victoria Shepherd. *(Pause. VICTORIA slowly and methodically tears her resignation into bits that she puts into the wastebasket. Then she picks up the telephone and dials.)*

My name is Victoria Shepherd. I want to file a complaint. *(Pause.)* Against my supervisor, Ms. Agnes Dudworth, and against Dr. Randall Ransom. *(Pause.)* Yes. I will come in to sign a complaint. I have one client to see. As soon as he leaves, I'll come to sign a complaint. Yes. A complaint against Ms. Agnes Dudworth, and Dr. Randall Ransom. Thank you. *(VICTORIA hangs up the receiver, walks to the office doorway, and calls in Mr. TULANE.)*

Mr. Tulane! I was expecting you! *(MR. TULANE enters with some sense of urgency. He has a letter of several pages in his hand.)*

MR. TULANE. Miss Vicky! We *won!* Look what came in the mail!

VICTORIA. We won?

MR. TULANE. We *won!* I'm to receive that money!

VICTORIA. Oh, the funds! You're to receive the money! Wonderful, Mr. Tulane!

MR. TULANE. You did it, Miss Vicky! *(Pause.)* Got these forms. Say first we have to fill 'em out and send 'em right back.

VICTORIA. We'll do that now!

TULANE. Yes, Miss Vicky. I *look* to you to make sure we get 'em right.

VICTORIA. I'll help, Mr. Tulane. We'll get them right.

MR. TULANE, *fondly.* Miss Vicky, what would I do without you?! *(Pause.)* Will you *always* be here to help me out?

VICTORIA. Why, Mr. Tulane! *(Embraces him.)* "Let's fight and press on to the end, then we may be victorious!"[23]

CURTAIN

Notes: The Stakes

1. Charlotte Leslau and Wolf Leslau, *African Proverbs* (New York: Peter Pauper Press, 1962, 1985), 21.
2. Julia Stewart, *African Proverbs and Wisdom* (New York: Kensington Publishing Corp., 1997), 57.
3. Leslau and Leslau, *African Proverbs*, 48.
4. Anonymous.
5. Vanessa Cross, *An Anthology of Black Folk Wit, Wisdom, and Sayings* (Kansas City, MO: Andrews and McMeel, 1994), 60.
6. Stewart, *African Proverbs and Wisdom*, 95.

7. Ibid., 150.

8. Ibid., 157.

9. Cross, *An Anthology of Black Folk Wit, Wisdom, and Sayings*, 19.

10. Ernest Gray, "Some Proverbs of the Nyanja People," in *African Studies Vol. 3, No. 3* (September 1944), 102.

11. Cross, *An Anthology of Black Folk Wit, Wisdom, and Sayings*, 29.

12. C. M. Dokes, "Bantu Wisdom-Lore," in *African Studies, Vol.6, No.3* (September 1947), 107.

13. Cross, *An Anthology of Black Folk Wit, Wisdom, and Sayings*, 52.

14. Ibid., 32.

15. R. Sutherland Rattray, *Ashanti Proverbs* (Oxford: The Clarendon Press, 1969), 190.

16. Cross, *An Anthology of Black Folk Wit, Wisdom, and Sayings*, 48.

17. Rattray, *Ashanti Proverbs*, 85.

18. Ibid.

19. Ibid., 97.

20. Ibid.

21. Cross, *An Anthology of Black Folk Wit, Wisdom, and Sayings*, 78.

22. Ibid., 57.

23. Rattray, *Ashanti Proverbs*, 97.

NOTES

NOTES

Abiona

A Play in One Act and Three Scenes

CHARACTERS
(In Order of Appearance)

MARGARET .... a social worker, African American, about thirty-five

JULIAN ....a registered nurse, African American, about twenty-four

LATIMER .... a psychiatrist, African American, late forties

BO RUTLEY........ boyfriend of EEDIE CONWAY, African American, twenty-eight

EDITH "EEDIE" CONWAY ....a patient, African American, twenty-seven

THE TIME
The present

THE PLACE
A psychiatric hospital anywhere in the United States

Scene One
Conference room. Morning.

Scene Two
Day room. Afternoon.

Scene Three
Conference room. Late afternoon.

SCENE ONE

SETTING:

The conference room of a psychiatric hospital. A large chalkboard with chalk and erasers faces the audience. On it is written:

PROBLEM LIST:
1. Confused, delusional
2. History of prostitution, petty theft

AT RISE:

MARGARET enters, writes "Resolved" opposite Problem #1, and adds more problems to the PROBLEM LIST:

3. *Substance dependence—alcohol (wine), cocaine*
4. *Immune disorder (HIV positive)*
5. *Needs special housing plan*

Just as MARGARET is completing #5, JULIAN enters and stares at the list for a moment before speaking.

JULIAN. We're staffing Edith Conway.

MARGARET. Right! Her life plan is due.

JULIAN. Some challenges! Look: alcoholism, cocaine addiction, homelessness, and now HIV. Eedie can *never* deal with all that!

MARGARET. But— *(LATIMER enters, glances at the Problem List, then sits down. Then he glances toward the window and sees EEDIE running.)*

LATIMER. Look! It's Eedie! She's training for the long run!

MARGARET. *(Goes to the window and is soon joined by the others. Crowd sounds.)* Great! They're coming round the bend! She's in front! Go Eedie, go! *(Rising crowd sounds.)*

JULIAN. Wow! That woman can kick up some dust!

MARGARET. Hold the lead! Go, Eedie! *(More crowd sounds. The treatment team members turn their attention back to the matter at hand.)*

JULIAN. She's *trying*. *(Pause.)* But running! That's like the old Eedie: always running!

MARGARET. Running's good!

JULIAN. I run track myself. But Eedie runs *away*.

MARGARET. I keep telling you: she's over all that.

JULIAN. *Every* time, she runs away and goes back to her coke-sniffing, thieving wine-head of a boyfriend.

MARGARET. Now her running's for Ogun, Lord of the Road.[1]

JULIAN. Ogun? Ha!

MARGARET. Ogun, Lord of the Road! She dedicated her running to him. She's even writing a poem about Ogun.

LATIMER. Ogun, Lord of the Road, god of wine, god of war, who finally warred with himself. Think she'll put that in her poem?

MARGARET. Ogun's war with himself? A most crucial point in the Ogun legend! Eedie's doing well in her study of the West African culture. She's committed to exploring her roots and wants to discover a new name for herself.

LATIMER. In the African culture names are given according to what happens when the person is born.

MARGARET. A new name! With us and Ogun, I know she'll do better.

JULIAN. Ogun? The war god? His name even *means* "war"! What can *that* do for Eedie?

MARGARET. A lot! Let's remember, he's not just a war god. He's Lord of the Road, god of creativity, of agriculture, the roof over the homeless, the—

JULIAN. Yes, Ogun's all that. But Eedie leaves here and is homeless over and over again. She gets out, guzzles wine, sniffs cocaine, and prostitutes, no matter what we do. So what can Ogun do? Besides, he got into trouble himself for being a wine-head.

MARGARET. Ogun learned from his mistake. And Eedie will learn from hers.

JULIAN. This time, besides being soaked in wine and cocaine, Eedie was lying on a busy street, crying for her dead mother.

MARGARET. But it'll be different!

JULIAN. And this time, she's diagnosed with HIV.

LATIMER. She absolutely must contact her partners!

JULIAN, *scoffing.* Think Eedie'll do that? She's a prostitute!

MARGARET. We're working on that.

JULIAN. She still lives with Bo. Has *he* even been tested? *(Pause.)* He steals, she prostitutes.

MARGARET. Eedie's growing up was rough. She was truant and fell in with the wrong crowd. Her mother, as a single working parent, struggled to cope. But her mother died just as she was taking a lead in plans for Eedie.

LATIMER. Eedie couldn't benefit from the planning while her mother was alive.

JULIAN. It was Eedie's choice!

LATIMER. Our job is to present her with better choices. Her interest in Ogun is a strong force. But does Eedie have the mettle? At least she's doing well for now—no more confusion, no more delusions, and— *(LATIMER's words are interrupted by loud shouts from the day room.)*

THE VOICE OF BO RUTLEY. Damn y'all, damn yuh! I'm gonna ... gonna ... see her! Yeah, gonna see Eedie. Now look-a-here, damn it ...! *(BO's slurred speech indicates he is drunk. MARGARET, LATIMER, and JULIAN all rush to the door, going into the day room, offstage. They return almost immediately.)*

JULIAN. Bo Rutley. That boyfriend of Eedie's!

LATIMER. Have him calm down, and then have him come in and talk with us.

JULIAN. Latimer! He's full of booze and who knows what else. He's creating a disturbance!

LATIMER. Let him come in.

JULIAN, *under his breath.* Call security and have him thrown out! *(Aloud.)* Let's stop this guy. He's drunk, and he's trying to intimidate staff!

MARGARET. Bo is a key person in Eedie's life. We're reaching out to him. Let him come in.

LATIMER. Of course we're here for him too, as well as Eedie.

JULIAN. This is the third time he's done this!

LATIMER. Come here drunk?

JULIAN. Yes, come here drunk! Thinking he can see Eedie! Thinks he can get his way by talking tough!

LATIMER. Well, let's speak with him. *(JULIAN goes and gets BO and escorts him into the Conference room.)*

MARGARET. *(Steps to the doorway and speaks to BO. BO enters, staggers some, clearly under the influence of street drugs and alcohol.)* Come in, Mr. Rutley.

BO. I ain't no *Mr.* Nobody! I'm just plain old Bo.

MARGARET. All right, Bo.

BO. Look-a-here! I know my rights! I gotta right to see my Eedie!

MARGARET. Visiting hours are in the afternoon. And you were told to visit only if you're sober.

BO. Yeah, yeah, they said that before.

MARGARET. Then why insist on—

BO. Well, see, I was close by. Don't make no sense to go back home; just have to come back later. I ain't got that kind of car fare!

JULIAN. You cannot come here drunk! That is the rule!

BO. I can't help what y'all's rules are! And I ain't even drunk! I just had, uh, a little sompn' to keep me goin'!

LATIMER. Mr. Rutley ...

BO. I already told you my name is Bo!

LATIMER. Bo, you'll have to leave now. When you come back, we'll schedule time for you to join Eedie and others in the family sessions.

BO. Now look-a-here: I gotta see my Eedie now!

JULIAN. Come back when you're sober.

BO. Just get one thing straight: *I* take care of Eedie—

MARGARET. Leave, Bo. Come back when you're sober! I'll be glad to talk with you. We want to help. (*BO leaves, showing defiant body language. JULIAN escorts BO out.*)

JULIAN, *returning.* Why we let that guy come here!

MARGARET. We can't keep Eedie from those she's close to.

JULIAN. He's an instigator!

LATIMER. But Eedie's run away without Bo. If it's not him, then it's some other reason. She's bound to run!

MARGARET. At times she's left on her own. But it's different now.

JULIAN. Different! Bo doesn't want help, yet Eedie's as close with him as ever!

MARGARET. Eedie's been with Bo a long time. It isn't easy.

LATIMER. Bo's still in Eedie's life, yet she wants a new life. *(Pause.)* Julian, is there a result from her testing?

JULIAN. Results show a bent for sports and an interest in study of other cultures.

LATIMER. Her interest in African cultures and names may point the way. And Ogun may help as well.

JULIAN. What's to happen when she leaves here?

MARGARET. Eedie's to live where there's help. She's going to Ogun's Road.

LATIMER. Ogun's Road. What sort of a place is it?

MARGARET. At Ogun's Road, they follow the philosophy of Ogun. It's a home where Eedie will get total care. They have medical care, therapy groups, crafts, vocational training, and more. She can rebuild her whole life.

JULIAN. Ogun's Road. Perfect! It's named for that drinking, warmongering god.

MARGARET. He's so much more! Why, he—

JULIAN. You think a fighting, drunkard god can help Eedie?

LATIMER. But Ogun learned. And Eedie can do the same. Margaret, what more can be said about Ogun's Road?

MARGARET. It's a warm, homey building surrounded by acres and acres of grassy meadow. A garden's in back, and there's a track field nearby.

JULIAN. The grassy meadow and track field might keep Eedie from running away!

LATIMER. Running away for Eedie has run out! Having HIV, she needs to get a new foothold.

MARGARET. Eedie has expressed that in our talks. And she's moved away from fear and self-blame, from feeling that now she must face her punishment: full-blown AIDS, and then death.

JULIAN. What's her focus now?

MARGARET. Her focus is on living. On living, and how it's to be for the rest of her life.

JULIAN. How does she want to be?

MARGARET. She wants her sobriety and her running. She wants to continue her study of her roots. (Pause.) And she wants a new name for herself.

JULIAN. Okay. But what about Bo? With Bo in her life, Eedie could change directions in the middle of the race! With Bo, all this that we're talking about ... *(There is a knock at the door. MARGARET steps to the door and finds EEDIE.)*

EEDIE. Good morning! May I come in?

MARGARET. Hello, Eedie! How are you this morning?

LATIMER. Good morning, Eedie.

JULIAN. 'Morning, Eedie! *(EEDIE enters the conference room. She is slim and casually dressed in running attire, athletic shoes, etc. Her speech lacks the correctness of LATIMER, MARGARET, and JULIAN, but is less coarse than BO's.)*

MARGARET. All right, Eedie. We're at a critical point.

EEDIE. You gonna let me go?

MARGARET. Are you ready?

EEDIE. Let me out of here!

LATIMER. You get out, then you come back.

EEDIE. It won't happen like before.

JULIAN. You always leave.

EEDIE. But not this time!

JULIAN, *looking at his watch.* Sorry. It's time for my next meeting. In fact, it's starting now. You can update me later. *(He exits the conference room.)*

MARGARET, *to EEDIE*. So, "not this time." That means you'll stay? What's the assurance you'll stay?

EEDIE. Stay on the road! I'm on the road now. Ogun had to stay on the road. And I'm stayin' on it too. *(She takes a wadded-up piece of paper from her pocket.)* This poem … I wrote it about Ogun. I gotta *write* his war, bit by bit as it comes to me.

MARGARET. We're listening.

EEDIE. I'm not nearly through with the poem. Little by little it shows up, and that's when I write it down.

LATIMER. Let's hear whatever words you have now.

EEDIE, *reading*.

> The great Ogun, god of war,
> Warrior god and King of Wine.
> With warlike foes he did spar.
> Still there came no victory sign.
>
> In spite of arrows, spears, and heat,
> Fierce battle on each side,
> Victory was a difficult feat.
> With neither team did triumph ride.
> It was said the two were tied.

MARGARET. The two armies are tied. Do they stay tied?

EEDIE. Seems like they're the same in bein' tough.

MARGARET. So how to break the tie?

LATIMER. Is there a tie *you* must break?

EEDIE. I'm tryin' to see ... still gotta see somethin'. *(She continues reading.)*

A lull came in the battle, a rest in the fight,
Between two armies of equal match.
Timeout to recreate the necessary might,
For neither side had borne a scratch.
Timeout to quench the thirst,
A rest in the battle royal,
For neither side had got the worst,
Despite much vigor and toil.

Ogun went alone to rest
In the shade of a glen
Wondering how to empower the zest
To let victory come to him and his men.

MARGARET. You stay on the road, Eedie.

LATIMER. So then what happens?

EEDIE. Gotta figure it out! Me and Ogun.

MARGARET. Stay with it, Eedie! It will come!

EEDIE. Ogun and me: both of us gotta stay on the road.

MARGARET. You can do it!

EEDIE. Oh, and there's this other poem, that's really about me!

LATIMER. What's it called?

EEDIE. "Give Me the Road!" That's the name of my poem: "Give Me the Road!"

MARGARET. We're listening!

EEDIE, *reading.*

Give me the road,
I need my space.
This right here ain't my place.
Give me the run, the speed, the air.
I really want to be out there.

I'll build my base,
Quicken my pace,
Train for the long run.
Oh, what fun!

I'll plant my heels 'gainst a strong support
To get my start and do this sport.

I'll catch the Sun,
Or make him run.

Bein' on the road is right for me,
That's the way I get to be free!

LATIMER. Why are you so anxious to leave, Eedie?

EEDIE. Let me out!

LATIMER. But how're you getting on?

EEDIE. It's okay.

LATIMER. Tell us about it.

EEDIE. Like my class in West African culture. We learned how African kids are named dependin' on things goin' on 'round the time they're born. And then some of us wanted to give ourselves African names. I couldn't think of a new name.

LATIMER. But the African practice is to name the *child*, the newborn, according to what happens around the time of birth. Doesn't apply to grown-ups.

EEDIE. I'm startin' a new life. It's somethin' like gettin' born.

LATIMER. Why not keep "Eedie Conway"?

EEDIE. Feel like I *passed* that lamppost. Now things are diff'rent.

MARGARET. Different?

EEDIE. "Eedie" is like bein' in a fog at the back of the pack.

MARGARET. You were in a fog?

EEDIE. The coke, the wine, the boostin', the hookin', and— *(Pause.)*

MARGARET. Yes, Eedie?

EEDIE. Well, Bo. And all that's about Bo.

MARGARET. And what's the feeling?

EEDIE. I'm thinkin', I've passed a few milestones, but now's time to surge to the finish line. You guys have worked real hard. All the plans. I wanna go to Ogun's Road. That's my chance. Chance for more forward moving. Chance to stay off coke and wine. Chance to start learnin' again. And this is my chance to try, so maybe this that's in my blood ... *(Pause.)*

MARGARET. You'll have it all, Eedie! You're building your mileage base.

EEDIE. But sometimes I'm not sure I can get there.

MARGARET. *Believe* you can get there!

EEDIE. Sometimes ... sometimes gettin' there seems so far away!

MARGARET. Believe in yourself, Eedie. Believe in yourself! You can do it! *(Pause.)*

LATIMER. But Eedie, what about Bo? Bo visits you every day.

EEDIE. He likes to see me often.

LATIMER. You and he must feel very devoted to each other.

EEDIE. You gotta understand ...

LATIMER. Bo's in touch with all that you want *now*?

EEDIE. Now don't go heapin' on Bo!

MARGARET. You think we're heaping on Bo, Eedie?

EEDIE, *squirming uncomfortably.* Well, me and Bo—it won't be the same with us.

LATIMER. Does Bo know that?

EEDIE. Sure, he knows!

MARGARET. How're you so sure?

EEDIE, *feeling caught.* Well, I hinted it to him.

MARGARET. You hinted it.

EEDIE. *(Pause.)* But maybe I should tell it to him in, uh ... a *stronger* way.

LATIMER. What'll you say?

EEDIE. Tell him I'm not the same like I used to be. Tell him now I need some stuff—stuff that don't go with stealin' and sniffin' and trickin'.

LATIMER. Anything else to tell Bo?

EEDIE. And that now ... now I got this HIV, gotta be careful. Can't do like I used to.

MARGARET. You're all for a change, Eedie.

EEDIE. A change!

MARGARET. Can you change and still have Bo in your life?

EEDIE. Me and Bo been together for years ...

MARGARET. Those years must seem like a long time.

EEDIE. Now I know I gotta let him go. I know that.

MARGARET. How is it—knowing that?

EEDIE. I'm gonna let him go real soft and easy.

LATIMER. When will you start to ... uh ... let Bo go?

EEDIE. Now I won't be rushed!

LATIMER. Still, you must decide.

EEDIE. But decidin' ain't easy. The first time I seen Bo I was sittin' in this bar. All by myself, and real wore out. Didn't know where I was gonna lay my head down to sleep that night. And then I seen Bo for the first time. I can see him now, comin' through the doorway, with that walk of his. Sure gotta walk, all right. He takes one look at me. And I look at him. And would ya' believe? It was like we been knowin' each other all our lives! He just looked at me, and I looked at him. And he's been lookin' after me ever since. So many years!

MARGARET. It's been a long time, Eedie.

EEDIE. And Bo's got some tender spots. I need time. I just need time. Can't rush, okay?

LATIMER. All right, Eedie. We'll talk it over at another time.

EEDIE. See y'all later. (*EEDIE leaves the conference room.*)

MARGARET. I think she needs a little more time. I'll keep you posted. (*MARGARET rushes after EEDIE.*)

SCENE TWO

SETTING:

Late that afternoon. The day room of the hospital. There is a small table for seating two persons.

AT RISE:

EEDIE is seated at the table. She is working on her Ogun poem. BO enters.

BO. Baby! *(He tries to embrace EEDIE.)*

EEDIE, *stiffly, clearly miffed.* Why'd ya come here drunk, Bo?

BO. I'm sober now, ain't I?

EEDIE. You were drunk! You were here drunk! You know that's against the rules!

BO. Aw, I just stopped to have a little sompn'.

EEDIE. You did it before. I keep tellin' you: you *can't* come here drunk!

BO. Now look-a-here, Eedie! Don't go gittin' all high and fine with me!

EEDIE. What you talkin' about?

BO. Gittin' all high and fine with me, 'cause you're *here*—here with these shrinks!

EEDIE. They ain't shrinks!

BO. Hey-y-y. Look like they about to turn your head. You gettin' just like em!

EEDIE. They're not like you make 'em out.

BO. Know one thing: they're against me. *(Pause.)* Now say it ain't so!

EEDIE. Margaret's been wantin' you to come talk with her.

BO. Not gonna set *me* down!

EEDIE. She wants to *talk* with you. See if you wanna stop drinkin' and druggin' and—*(Pause.)*

BO. Do I, sweetie? *(Laughs.)*

EEDIE. Oh, Bo! What's gonna happen to us?

BO. You gonna leave this place and come on back home. Just like before.

EEDIE. Am I, Bo?

BO. Where's my old Eedie? Where're your runnin' shoes?

EEDIE. They're not for runnin' away.

BO. Is that what the minks been tellin' you?

EEDIE. Don't call 'em names, Bo.

BO. They got names, honey, names that don't rhyme with Bo!

EEDIE. It-it's just ... they got different values.

BO, *mimicking.* "They got different values!" Now there you go! Talkin' like 'em!

EEDIE, *hurt.* Seems like whenever I come here, we're always fightin'. *(Pause.)*

BO, *tenderly.* I'm sorry, honey. *(Embraces her.)*

EEDIE. Always fightin'. Ogun would be fightin' too—

BO, *bored.* Not that war god again!

EEDIE. Bo, I'm writin' about Ogun for myself, and for you too. For both of us.

BO. I already heard 'bout Ogun fightin' and not winnin'—not losin', either—too much betwixt!

EEDIE. I'm still workin' on it. You gotta listen! *(She takes out the poem and prepares to read what she has written.)*

BO. Ogun's too wishy-washy— *(EEDIE stops BO with a sign and begins to read.)*

EEDIE, *reading.*

> A lull came in the battle, a rest in the fight,
> Between two armies of equal match.
> Timeout to recreate the necessary might,

For neither side had borne a scratch.
Timeout to quench the thirst,
A rest in the battle royal,

For neither side had got the worst,
Despite much vigor and toil.

Ogun went alone to rest
In the shade of a glen
Wondering how to empower the zest
To let victory come to him and his men.

BO. I already heard about that: Ogun can't make up his mind—can't win, can't lose! Just betwixt!

EEDIE. Try to see how Ogun was betwixt, and that's me too; I'm betwixt.

BO. I ain't betwixt 'bout *nothin!*

EEDIE. You gotta hear what happens next! *(BO shrugs, resigned. EEDIE reads.)*

Trickster god had watched the two armies spar.
Watched Ogun and his men fight with skill.
Though no victory fell to the God of War,
Trickster envied Ogun's strength and his will.

Old Trickster had not the power
To stop Ogun from winning the war,
Yet he plotted with each hour
How he might that victory mar.

To Ogun he went with a wine gourd in his hand.
"Brave Ogun, it's not too late,

You're the greatest god in all the land,"
Said Trickster god as he held the bait.

"Ogun, you great king, taste this brew!
See it sparkle! See it shine!
A sip of this will put you on cue:
You and your soldiers will win just fine."

Ogun shook his head,
"That won't do," he said.
"For I know where I'm weak,
As I know where I'm strong.
Wine I will not seek
For it does me much wrong."

With magic, old Trickster urged on
With flattery, praise, and crafty din,
'Til the will of Ogun was won,
And he finally gave in.

Ogun took one sip of the sparkling brew,
It gave his tongue a delight.
The blood in his veins was all ado,
His muscles were ready for the fight.

So he drank again and again.
The heat in his flesh was all joy.
The wine went down like torrential rain.
That drink was certainly no toy!

BO, *excited*. Ogun is *talkin'!* Naw, that drink *ain't* no toy!

EEDIE, continuing to read.

In the battle, Ogun and his men
Now fought with a might that was double.

Arrows that sped showed they would win,
Reduced their foes to rubble.

The battle was over in a brief span.
Arrows struck with the pull of each string.
Enemy not dead ran and ran.
Ogun and his men let victory ring.

Shouts went out for the war was won:
The enemy in flight,
A wreath for peace was spun.
Victory celebration was in sight.

BO. See? Victory! Wine won the battle!

EEDIE. But it's not over.

BO. Ogun *won!* Now he can drink some more wine!

EEDIE. That's not the end. Ogun won the battle, but—

BO. It's over!

EEDIE. It's not over. But I still have to find the words ...

BO. That is the end. Ogun drank that wine that was no toy. Then he won!

EEDIE. Bo ... *(Pause.)*

BO. You got sompn' to say?

EEDIE. Sompn' we gotta talk about.

BO. So talk.

EEDIE. Sompn' I gotta tell you.

BO. Go on. Say it, honey.

EEDIE. Bo. I- I can't go back to *livin'* like ... like that.

BO. Baby, they been fillin' your head with sewage. Sweetie, don't let 'em do that!

EEDIE. Been thinkin' a lot, Bo. Don't wanna go back to like before.

BO. Sweetie! After all these years ...

EEDIE. Don't wanna go back to smokin' rock, and drinkin', and hookin', and stealin'—

BO. Eedie, baby, these eggwits can't come between us. Don't let em!

EEDIE. Bo, I can't go back with you. This time, when I leave here, I'm gonna make a new life. Gonna go to Ogun's Road!

BO. Ogun's *what?*

EEDIE. I'm goin' to a swell place called Ogun's Road!

BO. Goon's Road!

EEDIE. But—

BO. No listen to me, Eedie: There's a deal goin' down. A *big* deal goin' down—

EEDIE. I won't hear nothin' about it!

BO. See, this deal, it's *big*. We—me and Pete—we been casin' the joint. After it's over—

EEDIE. I don't wanna hear 'bout no deal!

BO. I tell ya', Eedie, it's gonna be so *easy!* Me and Pete know the joint frontwards and backwards!

EEDIE. But—

BO. It'll be great, Eedie. After that, we have enough, you and me. We have enough so you're not on the streets. You and me.

EEDIE. I ain't goin' nowhere with you, Bo.

BO. Eedie, you gotta leave this place—like you did the last time, and the time before that. Like you *always* do.

EEDIE. I ain't gonna run away this time, Bo.

BO. Sure you will, honey. And your ol' Bo'll be waitin'.

EEDIE. Bo, it ain't the same no more.

BO. Sweetheart, ain't nothin' changed between us.

EEDIE. It's diff'rent now. *(Pause.)* It's in my blood.

BO. Blood? That's what the dung dips here tell ya'. Blood! But honey, you don't have to *believe* it!

EEDIE. It's true, Bo.

BO. That don't wind me up. Don't move me a bit!

EEDIE. *Let* it move you, Bo.

BO. Naw. Don't move me! Now the first time I heard it—this blood thing—thought it might *be* somethin'. So I went and got tested.

EEDIE. You *did*, Bo? You took the test?

BO. Took the test. And guess what, Eedie?

EEDIE. What?

BO. I ain't got it!

EEDIE. You ain't got it?

BO. Nah! Know what that means?

EEDIE. You lucky not to have—

BO. It means that since I ain't got it, then *you* ain't got it!

EEDIE. I got it, Bo.

BO. Naw. You must not, cause I ain't got it.

EEDIE. Bo, it don't have to work that way! I got it. I'm HIV positive!

BO. Okay. *(Pause.)* So all you gotta do is be real careful, Eedie. You know about that, don't you?

EEDIE. It's more 'n just bein' careful. Now I want my whole *life* to be diff'rent.

BO. You just been here too long. Too long in the nut house! So long in the nut house you get cracked! *(Laughs at his own joke.)* Oh, I know at first you had to be here, just like before. You was an ice block—didn't know the road from a crawdad hole! Needed to warm up. I couldn't warm you up. Hearin' them voices. Thinkin' you was Satan one minute, and Christ's angel the next. Babbling and slobbering. A block of ice. Nothin' wrong with gettin' your feet warm. *(Pause.)* But now it's time to move on.

EEDIE. But not *your* way.

BO. Baby, all you gotta do is leave. Get out of here. You done it before. Once you decide to leave, they can't hold you.

EEDIE. Bo ... I ...

BO. Do it, Eedie. Leave.

EEDIE. No. I—

BO. Do it. Get out of here.

EEDIE. But—

BO. I'll be waitin' for ya', Eedie. *(Bo lightly touches EEDIE's cheek and hair and slowly backs out, still talking.)* We're all waitin' for ya'. 'Member the last time we got zonked? You were all wild-eyed and dreamy. You had wings, and you were ridin' on a cloud. *(Pause.)* The best time we ever had. But this time we'll *really* celebrate. *(Pause.)* Got sompn' special for ya. Look, Eedie: it's snowin'. And we're gonna blow the snow. The best snow you can get. So much snow, we'll make snow angels. You'll be my snow angel. My angel in the snow. I'll be waitin' for you, Eedie. You just come and see. The best snow you can get. Savin' the best for my angel. *(Pause.)* I'll be waitin' for ya', Eedie.

EEDIE. *(She stands, watching BO leave, speaks again only after he has left the stage.)* Bo! *(She rushes after BO.)*

JULIAN. There are other clients, Margaret. We can't hang it all on any one client.

MARGARET. But Eedie was so motivated, so self-assured, so determined.

JULIAN. She let you down.

MARGARET. But I simply can't believe she ran away.

JULIAN. Look at her track record, Margaret. (*Pause. They all are lost in thought, silently brooding. Suddenly a weary, bedraggled figure enters, slowly drags herself toward MARGARET, JULIAN, and LATIMER. It is EEDIE. As she approaches the group, they stare in disbelief until she is facing them.*)

MARGARET. Eedie!

EEDIE. I couldn't do it.

MARGARET. So you came back.

EEDIE, *downcast.* I know what you all been thinkin'.

MARGARET. What are we thinking, Eedie?

EEDIE. Thinkin' I wasn't worth all the time you put in—especially you, Margaret. (*Looks at Margaret.*) You must think you worked for nothin'!

MARGARET. Eedie—

EEDIE. It's okay, Margaret. It's okay if that's what you been thinkin'. 'Cause I been thinkin' a lot too. (*Pause.*) After I went over the fence, and I was runnin' real fast, crossed that road, dodgin' cars, with you,

SCENE THREE

SETTING:

The conference room

AT RISE:

MARGARET and LATIMER arrive for the staff meeting, but JULIAN is not present. MARGARET writes the meeting agenda on the chalkboard thus:

1. *Nursing protocol*
2. *HIV/AIDS*

LATIMER. Where's Julian?

MARGARET. Wish he'd come on! Can't start the meeting without him.

LATIMER. We need his reports.

MARGARET. And there's the new AIDS Act.

LATIMER. Looks like Eedie's having a breakthrough.

MARGARET. So much has led to her maturing: the years of running, living on the streets, the HIV—

LATIMER. And Ogun has really played a role.

MARGARET. Ogun and her search for a new name have given her purpose and determination.

LATIMER. Now let's see what she does with all that.

MARGARET. Change is possible, even in a case like Eedie's. And then Julian'll learn too.

LATIMER, *looking at his watch.* Julian isn't usually late!

MARGARET. Where *is* he? (*As MARGARET finishes speaking, JULIAN enters. He is out of breath and disheveled.*)

LATIMER. Julian! What happened?

JULIAN, *panting.* It's Eedie!

MARGARET. Eedie? What happened?

JULIAN. She, she—

LATIMER. Yes?

JULIAN. She ran away!

LATIMER. Ran away?

MARGARET. Oh no! Ran away!

LATIMER. She ran away!

JULIAN. We tried to catch up with her. But— (*Makes a gesture of despair.*)

LATIMER. What happened?

JULIAN, *finally catching his breath.* Staff took her out on the patio in back. Took Eedie along with others, out for a few minutes of evening air. Eedie was near the fence, just taking in the breeze—or so it seemed. Then all of a sudden! (*Pause.*) I went over the fence behind her. But she was too fast. I couldn't catch up with her. She raced across the thoroughfare, dodging cars and trucks. (*Pause.*) But we lost her, guys. Once she was across that traffic, she disappeared among the buildings. (*Pause.*)

LATIMER. The race was almost won! Ogun's Road. A new life! (*Pause.*)

MARGARET, *visibly despondent.* What's the answer?

JULIAN. There are no easy answers, Margaret.

MARGARET. She was almost at the finish line. (*Pause.*) And we were there. Cheering her on. (*Pause.*) Once, when I saw Eedie run, I could see her discipline, her determination, in the set of her jaw and the beads of sweat rising on her skin. (*Pause.*) I saw that same discipline, that same determination in her race for a new life. (*Pause.*) And we were there, cheering her on. (*Pause.*) She was almost at the fini line.

JULIAN. You had great confidence in Eedie, Margaret. You believ her. You even inspired some of *us* to believe in Eedie.

LATIMER. Julian's right, Margaret. We all learned from your Eedie.

JULIAN. Sorry, Margaret. She couldn't marshal the speed.

MARGARET. It's the *endurance* that counts.

Julian, and the guards after me, I got to where there were buildings, close together, so I could run between 'em. That's when I got to thinkin'. And a cloud passed over my mind. And it was as if Ogun— Ogun out of my poem—was runnin' 'longside me. The black shiny muscles of his arms, his gray beard, his twinkly eyes. Ogun!

LATIMER. Ogun, who fought a battle, and couldn't win, and couldn't lose, either.

EEDIE. The two armies were tied, but then Ogun gets tricked into drinkin' wine. He *knew* that once he got started, he'd go on and on! He didn't mean to.

JULIAN. So does he win the battle?

EEDIE. (*She removes from her pocket the paper with the poem written on it and reads.*)

Shouts went out for the war was won:
The enemy in flight,
A wreath for peace was spun.
Victory celebration was in sight. (*Pause.*)

But to Ogun the triumph was strange:
His bow and darts he held tight.
He could not believe the change,
Couldn't believe there was not a fight.

Dreams twisted his vision, and he was not sane;
For in the end a spider pulled at his brain:

In his mind he relived the great battle
In his head the war didn't end,
In his thoughts there was never any peace. (*Pause.*)
In a moment of frenzy he slew his own men.

111

MARGARET. Killed his own men!

EEDIE, *reading.*

> Completely forgot these were his kin
> Who won the great battle with him at the head,
> Fought by his side
> And now they lay dead,
> Blood flowing from them, a mighty tide.

JULIAN. His very own kin that helped him win the battle!

EEDIE *(Nods sadly and continues reading.)*

> Ogun was found in whimpering grief.
> His own dead he buried, sad and forlorn.
> Of glory and peace *he* was the thief.
> He said, "Can I do no more than mourn?
> I've done an ill deed;
> Yet there's iron in my heart,
> Mettle is there for the life I must lead.
> Good deeds henceforth will be my part."
> Ogun stayed on the road
> But improved as much as he could.
> Followed a different mode.
> And tried to do good.
> For the homeless, a roof over their head,
> For the weary sick, a soothing balm,
> Food to eat and then a warm bed.
> Around Ogun all was calm.

> Iron he used to till his land,
> Grew plants and gave up strife,
> Grew healing herbs by his own hand,
> Worked to build a better life. *(Pause.)*

Those are the words that came to me as I was runnin'. Then I felt my legs turn around with my body movin' with 'em. It was like I was bein' carried. (*Pause.*) Ogun never said a word. But I could feel his thoughts passin' into my thoughts. So I knew I wouldn't run away no more. When he turned, I turned. And together we headed back. Once we got here, I couldn't see Ogun as much; he was fadin' away. He smiled and waved good-bye. Then he was gone. And I was here. So here I am.

MARGARET. Eedie, you're back!

EEDIE. Oh, by the way. 'Member I was tryin' to think of an African name for myself?

JULIAN. A name to stand for your life.

LATIMER, *to EEDIE.* You've decided?

EEDIE. As I was runnin', and with Ogun in my dream, somethin' kept whuppin' me. Then I remembered.

JULIAN. Remembered what?

EEDIE. I remembered the name "Abiona."[2,3]

JULIAN. "Abiona"?

MARGARET. You remembered the name "Abiona"?

EEDIE. Yes. Abiona. That's my name.

JULIAN. What's it mean?

EEDIE. It means "born along the road."

JULIAN. "Born along the road."

EEDIE. That's me: "Born along the road." *(Pause.)* I'm through runnin'!

CURTAIN

NOTES: ABIONA

1. Wole Soyinka, *Myth, Literature, and the African World* (London: Cambridge University Press, 1976), 29.
2. R. C. Abraham, *Dictionary of Modern Yoruba* (London: University of London Press, 1958), 6.
3. E. C. Rowlands, *Yoruba* (New York: David McKay Company Inc., 1969), 272.

NOTES

NOTES

GumBO

A Play in One Act

CHARACTERS
(In Order of Appearance)

MINNIE .... an African American woman in her thirties

DRUFORD .... an African American man in his forties

BO .... an African American man in his twenties

THE TIME
The present

THE PLACE
Interior of an addictions residential recovery
center anywhere in the United States

SETTING:

The day room of an addictions recovery home. This is a large living room with a kitchen area. A refrigerator and stove are in this area. A skillet is on the stove. A large bowl of okra sits on the porcelain part of the stove. A window with a curtain is near the stove.

Furniture in the room includes a larger table, a smaller table, three chairs, and a coat-tree. A mirror is on the larger table. A telephone is there also. A shawl hangs from the coat-tree as well as a red hat with feathers. In addition, a handbag hangs there. Also, DRUFORD's suit jacket and tie hang there. The smaller table is next to the chair where MINNIE is seated in the opening scene. A safe with combination lock sits in a corner of the room.

AT RISE:

MINNIE and DRUFORD are in the sitting room area. MINNIE is seated. She is sewing trousers for her child. On the table next to her are a chef's cap and matching apron that she has just finished sewing for BO.

DRUFORD is standing nearby, holding a clipboard on which he has lesson plans that he is working on, in preparation for the time when he can return to work as a schoolteacher. Having had more formal schooling than MINNIE, DRUFORD reflects this in his speech. MINNIE's manner of speaking suggests her formerly streetwise lifestyle, being less correct and polished than DRUFORD's.

MINNIE, *holding up tiny trousers she just finished sewing.* Look, Druford!

DRUFORD. They look great, Minnie.

MINNIE. Just the right size too. Left a little room here, and here, 'cause he's gotta grow,

DRUFORD. When are you going to see that boy?

MINNIE. Got a visit next week. They *gotta* let me see him for the holidays.

DRUFORD. You'll see him, no doubt about it! Hey, didn't you get some pictures?

MINNIE. *(Takes photos of her son from her pocket.)* Have a look.

DRUFORD, *looking at the photos.* Fine boy, Minnie!

MINNIE. They takin' real good care of him. He's gonna be strong!

DRUFORD. Like his ma, huh? You gonna teach him self-defense?

MINNIE. Self-defense? I don't think about that no more.

DRUFORD. What happened to all that good self-defense training?

MINNIE. Self-defense *used* to be necessary. It's different now.

DRUFORD. You forgot how!

MINNIE. I can't forget it, but—

DRUFORD. Bet you don't remember how to throw!

MINNIE. Bet I do!

DRUFORD. Come on! *(DRUFORD and MINNIE spar briefly. She throws him.)* Looks like you can still teach that little fellow something!

MINNIE, *smiling proudly.* I'm always thinkin' about him. I know it won't be long before he's back with me!

DRUFORD. It won't be long, Minnie. You'll get back.

MINNIE. I'm tryin' to get back. But so are you. Both of us tryin' to get back. How's your writin'?

DRUFORD. Lesson plans. Gotta have good lesson plans!

MINNIE. I'm always sewin'; you always writin' lesson plans.

DRUFORD. For when that time comes.

MINNIE. That time is comin', Dru. Time when you're with your students. Time when I'm back with my boy.

DRUFORD. You think the right time will come for Bo?

MINNIE. Bo? Hard to say.

DRUFORD. That's what I think. Hard to tell about Bo.

MINNIE. Bo says he's goin' to cookin' school when he's through here.

DRUFORD. Great cook. He's making us gumbo for our party tonight.

MINNIE. Says it's to show you, me, and Jake he's grateful for us puttin' up with him.

DRUFORD. Well, he could start with appreciation for this chef's outfit you made for him. *(Indicates chef's cap and apron.)*

MINNIE. Oh, he loves 'em, Dru! He said, "Thanks, Minnie. I been needin' a chef's outfit!"

DRUFORD. But when's he going to wear it?

MINNIE. Bo's been actin' kinda strange. Like he's got things on his mind.

DRUFORD. Jake noticed it too.

MINNIE. Hey, where *is* Jake, anyhow?

DRUFORD. He's visiting his family for the holiday. Says he'll be back in time for our little celebration.

MINNIE. Think he'll have us do the mirror dance?

DRUFORD. The mirror dance! Not at our holiday party!

MINNIE. Jake says we need to do that mirror dance every day.

DRUFORD. The mirror, every day?

MINNIE. To review our steps; see what works. *(She dances briefly.)*

DRUFORD. And what *doesn't!* *(He dances briefly, stumbles, almost falls.)*

MINNIE. Dance to the memory.

DRUFORD. Remember to keep time with your steps, or you fall. *(The telephone rings. MINNIE answers it.)*

MINNIE. Hello? Jake! *(Listens.)* Oh, Jake! I'm sorry to hear that! You gonna be okay? Sure, I'll tell Dru and Bo. But Bo went out. *(Listens.)* Yes, Dru's here. *(She covers phone receiver, turns to DRUFORD.)* Dru, it's Jake. Got a problem with his family. Gotta be out of town for a few days.

DRUFORD. Is he okay?

MINNIE. Says he can handle it. *(To JAKE.)* I told Druford you're gonna be away for a few days. *(Pause.)* Yes, Jake, I'll tell Bo. We'll be okay. Sure, I know this is the first time. *(Pause.)* Yes. I have the keys. And yes, I have the safe combination. It's in my head. *(Pause.)* Sure, Druford does all the writin'. *(Pause.)* Yes, Bo does the cookin'. He's the cook if you're not here. *(Pause.)* Yes, I promise: me and Druford'll take care of Bo. And you take care, Jake. Sure, we'll see to Bo. Don't worry, Jake. *(She hangs up.)* Imagine that! Jake gets called away just when we're about to celebrate for the holidays!

DRUFORD. Hard to imagine! All these months we've been together, and we're about to celebrate. Then he's not here!

MINNIE. Better for him to be with his family since they need him.

DRUFORD. He's gotta go where he's needed most. *(Pause.)* Wonder what Bo's going to think about Jake's being gone.

MINNIE. Hard to tell what Bo is thinkin' nowadays!

DRUFORD. Where *is* Bo, come to think of it?

MINNIE. Out buyin' cheese and chewin' gum.

DRUFORD. Cheese and chewing gum!

MINNIE. That's what he said: cheese and chewin' gum!

DRUFORD. I can understand the chewing gum. You know how Bo's got to chew—you know, those rocks on his back. But cheese? What's the cheese for?

MINNIE. That's what I told him! No way he had to go out and buy cheese! He was just a chewin' and a chewin' like always. Said "Minnie, you know how I gotta have my gum!" I said, "Sure, I know you gotta have your chewin' gum. But what about that cheese you gonna buy?" Then he claimed we need cheese to get us started—to get us all warmed up—'fore we taste his delicious gumbo.

DRUFORD. Bo ought to stop!

MINNIE. Think he really needed the gum. Just added the cheese, in case he decides to stay out longer.

DRUFORD. Must be that. Got everything for the gumbo right here. Shrimps, tomatoes, crab legs, and okra.

MINNIE. Know how ticky he is about that okra!

DRUFORD. Bo says it's the okra stickiness that really makes the gumbo!

MINNIE. The stickiness.

DRUFORD. It'll be a treat. Always a treat when Bo makes gumbo!

MINNIE. And he'll wear his new chef's outfit just for the occasion!

DRUFORD. A great time for him to get started with it!

MINNIE. You think Bo's gonna be okay? I mean with Jake gone …?

DRUFORD. Stop worrying about Bo, Minnie. He'll manage.

MINNIE. I do worry about that fellow. Can't help it.

DRUFORD. Aside from Bo, there are things we all need to remember now that Jake's gone.

MINNIE. Now you know Jake had already told us all what to do—just in case he had to be away.

DRUFORD. Sure, he prepared us. Now let's go back over it.

MINNIE. Let's see. Dru, you're the one that does the writin'.

DRUFORD. And Bo's the cook.

MINNIE. That leaves me. Remember what my role is?

DRUFORD. Why, you're the keeper of the safe. You're the one Jake trusts with the safe combination.

MINNIE. And I mean to be worthy of that trust.

DRUFORD. The safe combination! That's quite a trust. How do you manage all those numbers?

MINNIE. I got 'em all right up here. *(She indicates her head.)* Just right up here.

DRUFORD. Oh, there's no doubt you can handle it. It's no accident that the biggest responsibility rests on *your* shoulders.

MINNIE. So you see. It's all set. Everybody knows what they're supposed to do.

DRUFORD. Still, it's different, Jake's not being here. *(Pause.)*

MINNIE. You scared, Druford?

DRUFORD. This is the first time we've been by ourselves. Now wait; it doesn't mean I need Jake to be sure I don't do something I'd regret, but …

MINNIE. But?

DRUFORD. It'll just take some getting used to this first time.

MINNIE. Oh, we'll be okay. We haven't been here all this time for nothing!

DRUFORD. Wonder where that Bo is!

MINNIE. Out buyin' cheese and chewin' gum, I guess. But wonder what's takin' him so long!

DRUFORD. What'll we do about that mother instinct of yours?

MINNIE. What about *you*? Besides, gotta boy of my own! *He* takes care of my mother instinct!

DRUFORD. So what gives?

MINNIE. I just wonder: Was it really cheese and chewin' gum that took Bo out of here? Sometimes I wonder about that fellow.

DRUFORD. There you go again.

MINNIE. Hope he's not out buyin' somethin' *else!*

DRUFORD. Seriously, Bo seems unsure of what he's about.

MINNIE. Shaky, if you ask me.

DRUFORD. What should we do?

MINNIE. Same thing Jake has us doin' all along. Same thing we'd do if he was here.

DRUFORD. Come on. Say it.

MINNIE. The mirror.

DRUFORD. There you go again! The mirror!

MINNIE. The mirror dance.

DRUFORD. For the holidays. For our celebration?

MINNIE. You, me, and Bo could use some mirror time. 'Specially Bo.

DRUFORD. I keep thinking Bo's gotta change, after all that's happened to him.

MINNIE. He's had enough for a whole lifetime.

DRUFORD. After that *girl* ...

MINNIE. After that *fire* ...

DRUFORD. All those *scars* ...

MINNIE. No wonder he can't look in the mirror.

DRUFORD. He sees all the cracks.

MINNIE. You feel better once you learn to handle it.

DRUFORD. Honestly, Minnie. Sometimes Jake gets too deep. Doing the mirror—okay; but to add on top of that the *mirror*. (*Indicates actual mirror, which is lying on the table.*)

MINNIE. The mirror makes you *see!*

DRUFORD, *scoffing.* Still, it's the holidays!

MINNIE. Jake says he wants us to use our memories as stepping-stones, and how we've got to hold up the mirror to something.

DRUFORD. *(Mimics JAKE.)* Right. "'Hold the mirror up to nature'— with apologies to the Old Bard."

MINNIE. Yeah. That's how Jake says it: "Hold the mirror up to nature."[1]

DRUFORD. *(Stronger imitation of JAKE.)* "'Hold the mirror up to nature,' with apologies to the Old Bard."

MINNIE. That mirror pushes Bo away.

DRUFORD. Gets him all riled up.

MINNIE. Gets under all the scars. *(Pause.)* Dru—

DRUFORD. What's up, Minnie?

MINNIE. Somethin' on my mind, Dru.

DRUFORD. Let's see.

MINNIE. What if Bo was to take the wrong train?

DRUFORD. Where're you headed, Minnie?

MINNIE. If Bo forgot where he was goin' … and got on the wrong train?

DRUFORD. Of course we'd have to help him get back.

MINNIE. What if Bo's train derailed?

DRUFORD. We help him get back on track.

MINNIE. What if Bo didn't want it back on track?

DRUFORD. Then we'd have to let go, Minnie.

MINNIE. Let go, huh? Let go. *(She is visibly moved, feeling strongly that she could not let go.)*

DRUFORD. Nothing to do but let go, Minnie.

MINNIE. Let go. It's so easy to let go.

DRUFORD. Now look here, Minnie. I say sure, if Bo's train derails, we help him—or try to. But if the engineer doesn't want to get back, then there's no way we can force him.

MINNIE. Look at me, Druford. All three of us started together: you, me, and Bo. Together we decided which way to go.

DRUFORD. Sure. But I'm still me. You're still you. Bo's still him.

MINNIE. But this is different.

DRUFORD. How different, Minnie?

MINNIE. We gotta stick together, Dru. If one of us falls, the rest of us set him aright. If one train derails, the rest set it back on track.

DRUFORD. Even if the derailed one doesn't want it?

MINNIE. Even if! Think of how it was with you, Dru.

DRUFORD. With me?

MINNIE. Didn't you need to get back on track? Wouldn't that have been better, before it all exploded?

129

DRUFORD. Maybe. Maybe.

MINNIE. And take me. Didn't I need to get back on track before ... before ...?

DRUFORD. Look, Minnie. We all had something. We're here for that. Something brought us here.

MINNIE. Then promise. Let's promise each other, Dru: never, ever will we stand by and let any one of us fall. When we see that train derail, we go to the rescue.

DRUFORD. I'm with you, Minnie.

MINNIE. Remember how you once told us about those people, long time ago, that knew how to keep their promises?

DRUFORD. The ancients! Sure, the ancients made pacts.

MINNIE. Let's you and me make a pact like that.

DRUFORD. But with the ancients it was for a truce. That's not what's going on here.

MINNIE. What's happening here is we gotta be sure the *rest* of us won't let any *one* of us fall. *(Pause.)* Tell me again about the ancients, Dru.

DRUFORD. A warrior from each side poured red wine on the earth as a solemn promise.[2]

MINNIE, *nodding, as she remembers.* That the blood of whoever broke the truce would flow on the earth, just like the red wine flowed there.

DRUFORD. That the blood would flow just like the wine.

MINNIE. This is a pact, Dru. So beautiful. As fitting for us as it was for the ancients. Let's do that, Dru. The same way the ancients did. *(She goes to the cupboard, returns with grape juice she has taken from the cupboard.)*

DRUFORD. Minnie, put that grape juice back! We are *not* going to waste good grape juice!

MINNIE, *returning, indicating the grape juice.* Our symbol, our motto to stand by each other.

DRUFORD. I say okay! We agree. Don't waste—

MINNIE, *getting on with the ritual.* This table is the earth. And this that's in my hand *(indicates the grape juice she's holding)* is red wine. You pour, Dru. *(DRUFORD reluctantly takes the grape juice from MINNIE and pours some on the table.)*

DRUFORD. Okay. Feel better now that we did like the ancients?

MINNIE. Dru, this is our pledge. Our pact. This wine is our blood, our life force. The life force we use to not only take care of ourselves, but also to look out for others. If any one of us falls, the rest of us join forces to lift him up.

DRUFORD. We'll keep the pact.

MINNIE. While we keep *our* trains running. *(She hears a rumble in the corridor as BO is about to enter.)* Shhhhhh! *(BO opens the door and enters, carrying the small package of cheese and gum he went out to buy. He puts it on the larger table, then takes off his jacket and hangs it on the coat-tree. He is heavily scarred about the hands and face. He is chewing gum and may occasionally blow a bubble if it is bubblegum. Like MINNIE, BO lacks extensive formal education. His speech patterns are coarse compared to both MINNIE'S and DRUFORD'S, but are closer in structure and elocution to MINNIE'S than to DRUFORD'S.)*

BO. Got my gum, and I got the cheese, guys!

MINNIE. Bo, some unexpected news …

DRUFORD. It's Jake.

BO. Jake? What happened?

MINNIE. Trouble at home. He's gonna be gone for a few days.

BO. Sorry. Hope it's nothin' bad.

MINNIE. Jake says he can handle it. Just gotta be there.

DRUFORD. Which means he can't be *here*.

BO. So it's gonna be just the three of us.

DRUFORD. Just the three of us.

MINNIE. For the first time, just the three of us.

BO, *relaxing.* When the cat's away, the mice—

MINNIE. Uh, *these* mice *(indicates herself, BO, and DRUFORD)* play in a *different* way.

DRUFORD. They still get the cheese …

MINNIE. But without gettin' zapped in the trap! *(She and DRUFORD are dead serious, but she playfully pops a cheese nugget into BO's mouth.)*

BO, *noticing mirror on the table.* Why's this here?

MINNIE. That mirror?

BO, *with revulsion, since he dislikes mirrors.* This *mirror!*

MINNIE. Keepin' it handy for the mirror dance.

BO. Keep it handy. But don't put it in *my* hands!

MINNIE. Grab some okra, Bo. Cuttin' it up over here. *(BO walks to kitchen area where MINNIE is, and joins her in cutting up the okra for the gumbo.)*

BO. Druford and Minnie ...

DRUFORD. What's on your mind, Bo?

BO. I been thinkin' ...

MINNIE. So let's hear it.

BO. While I was out, passed by this place looked like one I used to know—long time ago.

DRUFORD. And?

BO. Got this hammerin'. Like old times. Like somethin' I tasted once. And bein' near the place, I almost could taste it again.

MINNIE. What did it taste like?

BO. Honey. Nothin' but honey.

DRUFORD. Now don't get any ideas, Bo.

BO. Tasted like honey. Nothin' but honey.

MINNIE. But the bees. What you think about that? The bees!

BO. Guys! It's the holidays!

MINNIE. The holidays. So on with our celebration!

DRUFORD. Come on. Put these on. *(Indicates chef's cap and apron.)*

BO. Later. Like I said: been *thinkin'*.

MINNIE. Yes?

BO. Been thinkin': bag o' rocks is real cheap. *(MINNIE shakes her head sadly.)*

DRUFORD. Now don't get stung!

MINNIE. Stay away from the hive!

DRUFORD. Don't get stuck!

BO. For the *holidays*.

MINNIE. Bo, we mean to climb to the top of the hill. Don't roll that ball up the hill only for it roll back down again.

DRUFORD. Keep that ball at the top of the hill, Bo.

BO. Just one hit. Just for the holidays.

DRUFORD. One hit. And you hit rock bottom.

MINNIE. Why fall and hit rock bottom?

BO. But those rocks could rock me to sleep.

DRUFORD. They keep you at the bottom.

BO. For the holidays! Just once, for the holidays.

DRUFORD. But Bo—

BO. I'll stop after just one bag. That's all I need. Don't tell me I can't stop. I know my own mind. I know my own will. I will use, and I will stop. I will!

MINNIE. You lookin' for a thrill? Then quick, make a will!

DRUFORD. You are much too willful!

MINNIE. Have some willpower!

BO. I tell you, guys: I can still be clean after a little celebration. Easy. Just like I can get my girl Eedie back.

MINNIE. When you turn it all around!

BO. Anytime! All I do is beck my little finger, and she—

DRUFORD, *scoffing.* But she didn't.

MINNIE. You been goin' up there, Bo. Always after Eedie. But—

DRUFORD. She knows what she wants!

BO. Just like I get them rocks off my back, I get my Eedie back! *(Pause.)* Why she left me!

MINNIE. You had bees in your brains. And the honey pot wasn't sweet no more!

DRUFORD. Give yourself some time, Bo. It'll work out.

BO. I know you guys are just tryin' to help me. I know that.

DRUFORD. Then let us see it, Bo. We need to *feel* it!

BO. Feel it? Naw, you gonna *taste* it! I'm cookin' tonight, remember?

MINNIE. You makin' gumbo.

BO. Right. Gumbo it is! And you know why it's gumbo I'm makin'?

DRUFORD. Why?

BO. It's for the two of you. For Druford and Minnie. *(Pause.)* Minnie, you're both a mother and a friend to me, all in one. *(Pause.)* And it was you, Dru, who taught me how gumbo is an African word meanin' okra. I been eatin' gumbo all my life, but I never knew that. Then you said it. I never heard that before: gumbo, a Bantu word meanin' okra; gumbo, an African word for okra.[3] Then I remembered how gooey and sticky okra is when I pop it in the soup. And then how you—both of you, Druford and Minnie—want to stick to what we're about. How you want *me* to stick to what we're about. So I thought I'd make us gumbo for the holidays to show that just like okra is sticky, we can stick to what we're tryin' to do.

MINNIE. Then *be* like gumbo. Stick with what you gotta do!

DRUFORD. That is the sticking point!

BO. Gottta go, guys!

DRUFORD. And lose all you worked for?

MINNIE. Bo, you don't mean that!

BO. Just for the holidays, that's all. Just for the holidays, just a little celebration ...

DRUFORD. Got our party right here.

MINNIE. Got all we need.

BO. Y'all can't do like me. Take me, now: I can use, and after, I'm still okay.

MINNIE. You go backwards!

BO. I'll still be clean. I can do it, and when it's over, I'm still clean like it never happened.

MINNIE. Why'd ya' come here, Bo?

BO. Why'd I come here?

MINNIE. Sure. Why'd you come here? Why're you here, if you can go out and tiddly wink, and still you think you're clean?

BO. I need a place to stay.

DRUFORD. No.

BO. That's it. Just need a place to stay. Just out of the hospital. No job. These scars. Need a place to stay.

MINNIE. Dibbledabble!

DRUFORD. Come clean, Bo.

BO. I *am* clean. I can use. Still be clean.

DRUFORD. Bo—

BO. Just for the holidays. I can use. Come back. Still be clean.

MINNIE. Remember that girl, Bo. Remember Eedie.

DRUFORD. She couldn't stay.

MINNIE. She left, Bo.

DRUFORD. Had to.

MINNIE. Had to find a new life.

BO. Eedie never really left.

DRUFORD. She's gone.

BO. All I gotta do is go up there—

DRUFORD, *scoffing.* You've *been* up there!

BO. I beck my finger, and—

DRUFORD, *still scoffing.* Queen bee flew the nest!

MINNIE. Don't go out there, Bo.

BO, *grabbing his jacket and heading toward the door.* I'm goin'!

MINNIE. Remember the fire, Bo!

BO. *(Stops in his tracks.)* What?

MINNIE. The fire! The fire!

BO. Now, wait!

MINNIE. The scars, Bo! Remember the scars! *(MINNIE and DRUFORD try to get BO to look at himself in the mirror.)*

BO. Y'all heard me! Don't need no ritual! *(He pushes the mirror away. He takes further steps toward the door, but MINNIE rushes ahead of him and physically blocks his exit.)*

MINNIE. Bo!

BO. Out of my way, Minnie! *(She tries to push him away from the door.)* Get off me, woman! *(He tries to push MINNIE aside. DRUFORD rushes up. MINNIE and DRUFORD struggle with BO to prevent him from leaving.)*

DRUFORD. Easy goes it, Bo. Easy, Bo. *(DRUFORD and BO struggle, but BO wrestles DRUFORD to the floor, pins him down.)*

BO. So! What you think you doin' tryin to stop me from what I want? Try that again and get more of the same. *(BO is triumphant astride DRUFORD but fails to see MINNIE moving toward him. She takes him down with a swift karate move. DRUFORD, injured slightly, struggles up. Together MINNIE and DRUFORD restrain BO and remove his money, keys, and shoes.)*

MINNIE. Money! Keys! *(She tosses BO's money clip and keys toward the safe.)* Now the shoes! *(She struggles to remove BO's shoes with BO squirming as DRUFORD holds him down.)*

BO. Let go, Minnie and Druford! Let me up, I say!

MINNIE. One shoe! *(She succeeds in freeing one of BO's shoes, tosses it toward the safe, then works on the other shoe.)*

BO. My money! My shoe! Give 'em back! My keys!

DRUFORD. The safe.

MINNIE. Now the other shoe. Then all in the safe.

BO. Get your meddlin', grubby hands off me! *(He struggles, but DRUFORD has a strong hold on him. DRUFORD and MINNIE remove his other shoe and toss it also toward the safe.)*

DRUFORD. Quick, Minnie, in the safe! *(MINNIE quickly does the safe combination, tosses BO's things in, including his jacket, which fell on the floor during the struggle.)*

MINNIE. Got it all?

DRUFORD. Not going anywhere now.

BO. Damn ya'! To hell with both of you! Rot in hell!

DRUFORD. All okay now, Minnie?

BO. Fools!

MINNIE. Yep! Got 'em all locked up in the safe! *(DRUFORD lets BO up.)*

BO. Damn fools! Gimme my stuff, Minnie!

MINNIE. The mirror dance!

BO. Ya'll oughtn't a-done what ya' did!

DRUFORD. The mirror.

BO. The mirror? Take my stuff, then talkin' bout the mirror?! Gimme my stuff! Hear, Minnie? My stuff!

DRUFORD. The mirror will keep us all on track, Bo.

BO. My train stays on track!

MINNIE. Stop putting roadblocks on the rails.

BO. Just a little oil to smooth out the journey.

DRUFORD. Gotta know where your train is going, Bo.

BO. I know where my train's goin'!

MINNIE. You *forget* where it's supposed to go.

BO. I know what I want. Know what I can do. Know where I'm goin'! Gimme my stuff!

MINNIE. The mirror dance. Just like when Jakes's here.

BO, *scoffing.* The mirror? *(Pause.)* Gimme my stuff!

MINNIE. Remember, Bo. Remember ...

DRUFORD. Remember the fire.

BO. What?

MINNIE. Remember what happened.

BO. Minnie, since you're so bent on *me* doin' the mirror, then *you* do it!

MINNIE. Me? But—

BO. Do it, Minnie. Do the mirror.

DRUFORD. Bo's right, Minnie. Start with you. You can take the lead, and show the rest of us how.

MINNIE. But I'm not about to fall.

BO. Anyone can fall.

DRUFORD. Come on, Minnie. Start us off. The mirror.

BO. Remember heroin, Minnie. (*DRUFORD leaves the scene as unobtrusively as possible.*)

MINNIE. Heroin is my friend. Heroin is my lover. I want to marry heroin.

BO. What do they call you?

MINNIE. Heroin Hattie! They call me Heroin Hattie! (*MINNIE has gotten into character to play herself as she was before she entered Recovery House. She puts on the red hat.*)

BO. Heroin Hattie. But you're also Minnie. And Minnie has a child. (*MINNIE removes hat and mimes rocking the infant she has quickly shaped from the shawl hanging on the coat-tree nearby. BO narrates MINNIE'S story.*)

This gift, this jewel, this flower of your womb. (*As BO narrates, MINNIE mimes: she kisses the CHILD, gently puts him in cradle, etc. Then she puts on makeup and prepares to go out into the night.*)

You leave him to slip out into the night. (*"The night" is an adjoining area of the stage, apart from where MINNIE and her CHILD have their home. MINNIE slips out to sell drugs and prostitute. DRUFORD enters as CUSTOMER, cap on backward, intoxicated and swaying.)*

Heroin Hattie! Sell it from your hat! Feathers curled up hold more than a pack of precious gems for a life carefree. *(MINNIE sells CUSTOMER drugs. CUSTOMER snorts the substance, gets high.)*

Caught in the snare of traffic in thrills, all you want is to collect those bills. You fight to survive. Smoky haunts keep you alive, feed the gnawing hunger, fill the burning pit. *(Pause.)* You *can't* quit! *(MINNIE injects herself with heroin as CUSTOMER snorts cocaine.)*

Got a habit, can't help yourself. Addict sells to addict tryin' to stay "strong"! *(BO speaks mockingly. MINNIE and CUSTOMER mime to correlate with content of BO's narration.)*

They come to sample the merchandise. Hunger is a magnet that bites like a vise.

(MINNIE picks up a john played by DRUFORD. They go off arm in arm, leave the stage. MINNIE returns alone, goes to her CHILD.)

You let it all go. And not so slow. He *(indicates the CHILD) can't* grow. *(MINNIE lovingly tends to her CHILD.)*

You leave your life of the night, go home to do somethin' right. But you keep steppin' to a double beat. *(Pause.)* Mama tippin' out to work in the night, baby left alone ... *(MINNIE mimes continually stealing out into the night to sell and use, then returning to her CHILD.)*

But wait. *(Pause.)* That dreadful knock on the door. *(There is a firm, authoritative knock at the door. THE STATE enters, played by DRUFORD. He wears a dress hat and suit jacket.)*

DRUFORD as THE STATE. Ma'am, the State is taking custody of the child. *(MINNIE, clutching the CHILD, backs away.)*

MINNIE. No!

DRUFORD as THE STATE. We warned you! The State has come for him.

MINNIE. But I—

DRUFORD as THE STATE. We warned you time and time again ...

MINNIE. Please!

DRUFORD as THE STATE. We warned you not to leave him alone.

MINNIE. I *didn't*—

DRUFORD as THE STATE. Too many times he's been hurt when you left him alone.

MINNIE. Please! I won't do it again! *Don't* take my baby!

DRUFORD as THE STATE. Give me the child, ma'am. The State is taking custody.

MINNIE. No! *(In the course of the exchange with THE STATE, MINNIE desperately clutches the CHILD closer to her, backs away from THE STATE, as he gradually approaches her.)*

DRUFORD as THE STATE. Give me the child. *(He takes the CHILD from MINNIE and immediately leaves with him. Devastated, MINNIE collapses into a chair, sobbing.)*

BO. So that's the tale of Heroin Hattie! All she wanted was to get real high, to give herself a shot in the thigh, to feel like she was on top of the sky! Let it all go up in smoke, wouldn't stop till the bubble broke! *(Pause.)* Now where's your high, Ms. Heroin Hattie? Was your cravin' worth all that ravin'?

MINNIE. *(She's herself again.)* My son won't be away forever.

BO. So what's gonna happen?

MINNIE. I'll get him back. I will!

DRUFORD, *returning to the scene.* You can do it, Minnie. You'll get him back!

MINNIE. I can, and I will! *(Pause.)* Bo, come on. Get out here.

BO. Not me. I packed up all my memories.

MINNIE. But what about that girl?

DRUFORD. And that fire?

MINNIE. And what about—

BO. I said, Not *me!* This mirror, that ceremony just ain't for me.

DRUFORD. Then where is the light?

BO. The mirror is for people that still have stuff inside 'em they gotta sift out.

MINNIE. So let the light shine. We'll help you.

BO. I gotta get these rocks off my back. Come back. Still be free.

DRUFORD. Let the mirror show the way.

BO. Druford, take a look at yourself, not me. Take a good hard look at yourself. Hold up the mirror ...

DRUFORD. I can, and I have. I have taken that look.

BO. Where's that school you had? Where're the kids?

DRUFORD. You point to me, when *you're* the one that goes rotting about.

BO. I'm not gonna rot about no more.

MINNIE. Let him be, Druford. Bo's right. *You* do the mirror.

DRUFORD. I don't have to bare my chest just to show the hairs on it.

MINNIE. The mirror is like self-defense trainin'. Muscles get firm. Muscles you didn't even know you had. *(DRUFORD moves to where his tie and jacket are hanging, puts them on, gradually getting into character as MINNIE begins to narrate. BO quietly leaves the scene.)*

(Narrating DRUFORD's story.) You were a model of perfection. The purest essence of the school master. Your students looked up to you. Their parents looked up to you. Your peers looked up to you. For you had a message. When you talked, they all listened.

DRUFORD. *(He is in the character of the school teacher he once was.)* Boys and girls, I speak to you today as I would to my own sons and daughters: Don't answer the call of the street corner. Follow the path of your highest aspirations. That path has been landscaped by powerful forces. Tend it. For there lies your garden. Create paths for the flowers of your ambitions to gloriously bloom in. And let that aspiration be your civil engineer. Let your corners be square.

THE STAKES: THREE PLAYS OF THE BLACK EXPERIENCE

But don't hang out on them. Pave your roads with dreams. But not the dream of the easy high. (*The audience becomes DRUFORD's classroom. He moves closer to the audience as he speaks.*)

MINNIE. 'Member when you were tellin' me and Bo about those people long time ago tryin' to obey two different gods at the same time? (*BO enters in character of DOPE SELLER.*) Trouble is, whatcha gonna do when one god disagrees with the other? (*DRUFORD quickly looks around to be sure no one is watching. Then he buys cocaine from the DOPE SELLER, takes a long snort, relaxes, quickly composes himself, and returns to his class.*)

DRUFORD. Tommy, you want to be an astronaut. Do it. Hang on to your dream. Be ready to launch. Let your ship arrive at a true desire. You have a dream. Make for a smooth liftoff. Don't let drugs be your launching pad. Don't blast away on dark particles. Don't get spaced out. Build a strong space station. Let it be a starship. A star to light you away from the darkness that makes dreams die. (*Pause.*) Sandra, you want to serve your fellow creatures. Such a noble desire! You want to serve the oppressed, the downtrodden, the wronged. (*Pause.*) So don't wrong *yourself* for the easy high. Keep your dream strong! (*Pause.*) For you are the butterfly. But you're also the chrysalis. Just as the chrysalis nurtures and protects the butterfly, so will you nurture and protect your fellow creatures, to hold them, to guide them, until they're ready to soar. And you will soar. Don't let dark habits clip your butterfly wings. Don't let your chrysalis be cracked by the contraband dealer. For without it, there can be no butterfly. And Ellen, you want to be a jazz musician. Well, play that trumpet. Play it loud. Play it long. Sing old Gabriel a note for his money! Junk in your veins won't craft the tune. At this very moment, you have all you need to breathe life into your dream. (*DRUFORD now turns his attention to the entire class.*)

(*Rapping.*)

Think you want some weed?
Plant, boys and girls.
But that ain't the seed.

Got cocaine on your brain?
Are you insane?

Wanna buy a bag?
Don't be a rag!

Think heroin's your cue?
It'll make you blue.

Don't shoot up.
That won't win you a cup!

MINNIE. But the truth came out! Lit up like a spark! As others found out what you did in the dark! *(BO enters in the character of one of DRUFORD's students. He prances around DRUFORD, teasing him. DRUFORD is ashamed, hides his face in his hands, tries to get away, but can't, for at every turn he is confronted by the teasing character being played by BO.)*

BO. Teach does coke! Teach does coke! Teach does coke! *(BO prances rapidly around DRUFORD in a teasing, childlike manner.)*

MINNIE. No hidin' place, Dru. No place to hide your face. *(DRUFORD and BO have resumed their usual characters.)*

BO. You let 'em down, Dru.

MINNIE. Dru, you gonna have a new life.

DRUFORD. I'll get another school. Things'll be different. See? I'm even working on these lesson plans.

MINNIE. Bo, it's your turn now.

DRUFORD. Come on! Let's go!

BO. Not me!

DRUFORD. Minnie and I have danced our memories. Now your turn.

MINNIE. What steps you gonna show us?

BO. Not me. I had too much of that already.

DRUFORD. Remember Jacob's fight with the angel.

BO. All I'm saying is it's time for me to move forward. This mirror thing
don't allow that.

DRUFORD. Remember Jacob said to the angel, "Let me go!"

BO. That's it! This mirror thing gotta let me go! And y'all gotta let me go!

DRUFORD. And the angel said, "I'll only let you go after you have
blessed me."

BO. Aw, naw. That's not what I mean!

MINNIE. Dru's right, Bo. Cuddle up close to the troublin' things, and
look 'em in the face!

DRUFORD. Remember that girl, Bo. Remember Abiona.

BO. Abiona? Abiona's just a name Eedie took when she thought she had
"found" herself. (*His attitude is that of scoffing at the idea of EEDIE
wanting to "find" herself.*)

MINNIE. She must want to be a new person.

BO. Still, to me, she's just Eedie. Just my Eedie.

DRUFORD. But where is she?

BO. Eedie wanted a change.

MINNIE. Did she want *you* to change?

BO. I was still boozin' and druggin'.

MINNIE. What happened after she left?

BO. I was lost.

DRUFORD. You had to decide what to do next.

BO. I didn't know what to do. I was shut down. Dead.

MINNIE. You still had to decide.

BO. I thought if I could stop boozin' and druggin', then me and her could get back.

DRUFORD. You make it sound so simple.

BO. I tried. Even got a job.

MINNIE. You tried. Got a job. And then what?

BO. That's it. That's what I did.

DRUFORD. Tell us what else you did, Bo.

BO. I said that's it!

DRUFORD. You did something else, Bo.

BO. I said that's it!

MINNIE. You moved back home with your mother! That was the next thing you did.

DRUFORD. That's what you did, Bo. You moved back home with your mother. *(Pause.)*

BO. Back home things might get straight. *(MINNIE acts the part of BO's mother. She may place around her shoulders the same shawl previously used to create the CHILD. She takes the handbag that is hanging from the coat-tree.)*

MINNIE as BO's MOTHER. Son, you're back home!

BO. I'm glad to be back home, Mama.

MINNIE as BO's MOTHER. You're going to be good now?

BO. Yes, Mama. Gonna do nothin' but good.

DRUFORD, *narrating.* Indeed, you were good. For a while.

BO. I'm goin' to work now, Mama. *(BO exits, leaving for work.)*

DRUFORD. Your mama was so happy! So full of hope! You were back home. You had a job. You were going to be good! *(BO returns from work, hands his paycheck to his MOTHER.)*

BO. Got paid today, Mama. You keep it for me.

MINNIE as BO's MOTHER. That's a good son, Bo! Bringing your paycheck home to your old mother!

BO. Want it in safe hands, Mama.

DRUFORD. Safe hands conquer the tempting demons. *(Pause.)* For a while.

MINNIE as BO's MOTHER. *(She looks inside handbag, finds money gone.)* Bo, did you take some money out of this bag?

BO. Naw, Mama. I didn't take nothin'.

MINNIE as BO's MOTHER. But it was *here*, Bo! The money was *here!*

BO. I *told* you, Mama! I didn't take *nothin'!*

MINNIE as BO's MOTHER. But the money was here, Bo. It was right here in this bag.

BO. I told you, Mama: I didn't take it!

MINNIE as BO's MOTHER. It was here, Bo.

BO. You always blamin' me. Blame me for everything!

MINNIE as BO's MOTHER. Bo, you were going to try and be good. *(MOTHER exits the scene.)*

DRUFORD. That old craving! *(BO looks around to be sure he's not being watched. Then he takes money from his MOTHER's purse, which has been left nearby. He pantomimes going out and buying cocaine, takes a deep snort, relaxes in a kind of ecstasy, pulls a whiskey bottle from his back pocket, takes a drink, wipes his mouth with the back of his hand. Then he swaggers home.)*

MINNIE as BO's MOTHER. Money's gone again, Bo.

BO. I ain't took nothin', Mama.

MINNIE as BO's MOTHER. You're drunk!

BO. Nothin' wrong with me!

MINNIE as BO's MOTHER. Bo, you've got to get help.

BO. I'm all right, Mama.

MINNIE as BO's MOTHER. You can't go on like this.

BO. I'll get some help, Mama. (*MOTHER exits scene.*)

DRUFORD. But those old habits! (*BO pantomimes continuing to steal from the household funds, slipping out, and using street drugs and alcohol.*)

Time comes when the daily dose cannot appease the hungry cup. (*BO sets up freebase apparatus. He heats cocaine powder and baking soda on the stove, but doesn't notice when a spark causes the curtains to catch fire. He puts heated substance into a pipe, which he smokes. BO gets more and more intoxicated, takes no notice as the room fills with smoke.*)

You set machinery going to get a real high. But danger was nigh. You got drunker and drunker. You had a monkey to feed. Smoke filled the room, but you paid it no heed. Curtains went up in flames. (*BO finally notices the smoke and flames, tries desperately to put fire out, staggers about clumsily, trying to put out the fire, but he is too intoxicated.*)

When you finally saw the smoke and flames, it was late. There wasn't time. (*Pause.*) And then—

MINNIE as BO's MOTHER, *offstage, coughing and choking from the smoke.* Bo! Bo!

BO, *drunkenly groping about.* I'm comin', Mama!

DRUFORD. But you couldn't.

MINNIE as BO's MOTHER. *(She crawls into the scene, gasping and coughing, as the siren of a fire truck is heard in the distance.)* Bo! Help! Help!

BO. Mama! I'm comin', Mama!

DRUFORD. But you were too intoxicated, too inebriated ... *(BO frantically, helplessly, stumbles about in a stupor, reaches out for his MOTHER.)*

BO. *(He reaches out for his MOTHER as she is dying.)* Mama! Mama!

DRUFORD. It was too late for your mother. *(BO loses consciousness. His MOTHER dies. She rises and backs off the stage. Pause. BO is back in his character of the present. He is crestfallen, quite overcome with his reenactment of his experience. He slowly moves toward the mirror, looks in it, lightly touches the burn scars on his face and hands. MINNIE enters as MINNIE.)*

MINNIE. Bo, you wanted to go out ... *(She walks to the safe.)*

BO, *wearily, half dazed.* What ya' doin', Minnie?

DRUFORD. You wanted to go out, Bo.

MINNIE. We can't stop you from doin' what you want.

DRUFORD. Your things: your shoes, your money, your keys, your jacket ...

MINNIE, *removing BO's things from the safe.* You have a right to your things, Bo.

DRUFORD. Nobody can stop you from doing what you want. *(BO takes his things that MINNIE is offering him and puts on his shoes.)*

MINNIE. You can leave now, Bo. *(BO moves slowly toward the door, hesitates, comes back, takes his jacket, which he has left on the table, and again moves toward the door. He is having an inner struggle. Trying to look determined and defiant, he puts on his jacket. He again moves toward the door. Arriving there, BO puts his hand on the doorknob. But then he suddenly turns back.)*

BO. Wait. *(Pause.)* Sompn' about gumbo!

MINNIE and DRUFORD. Gumbo? *(MINNIE and DRUFORD exclaim in unison, registering genuine surprise.)*

BO. Sompn' about what gumbo means.

DRUFORD. "Gumbo" is an African word meaning "okra."

MINNIE. And you said okra is sticky.

DRUFORD. And you said gumbo reminds us to stick to what we're about.

MINNIE. The sticking point!

BO. But somethin' else sticky just popped in my head!

MINNIE. What else just popped in your head?

BO. "Gumbo's" got "gum" in it. Now, gum is sticky.

DRUFORD. Gum is sticky. So? *(DRUFORD and MINNIE still don't get BO's point.)*

BO. Sticky as gum is, it's got *Bo* in it. *(Pause.)* Git it?

MINNIE. So "gum" and "Bo" join up to make gumbo. *(MINNIE and DRUFORD are just getting BO's point.)*

BO. Right! Git it? "Gumbo" means "Bo sticks like gum!"

DRUFORD. Then let's all be sticky like gum, just like Bo!

BO. Right. We gonna stick together. And Bo's gonna show how he can stick with it—be as sticky as okra, sticky as gum!

MINNIE. Gum. Bo. Okra. Gumbo. It all sticks together! *(BO hangs up his jacket, signaling he has no intention of going out.)*

BO. Hey, guys, where's the party?

MINNIE. Let's have some music!

BO. Great! And where's my chef's apron?

DRUFORD. Got it right here, Bo. *(DRUFORD and MINNIE help BO put on chef's apron. Then BO kneels, and MINNIE ceremonially crowns him with the cap.)*

BO. I'm gonna make the best gumbo anybody ever wet their gums on!

MINNIE. The best ever!

DRUFORD. Wait'll Jake gets back!

MINNIE. He won't *believe* what he's been missin'!

CURTAIN

NOTES: GumBO

1. William Shakespeare, "Hamlet, Prince of Denmark" in *The Complete Pelican Shakespeare*, Act III, scene ii, ed. Willard Farnham (Baltimore: Penguin Books, 1969), 952.
2. Homer, *The Iliad*, ed. Rev. W. Lucas Collins (Philadelphia: J. B. Lippincott Co., 1878), 60.
3. *Webster's New World Dictionary and Thesaurus* (New York: Simon and Schuster, 1996), 274.

NOTES

e Author

...ker, teacher, and award and grant-winning ...ay-Séré created this exciting new collection, the Black Experience to Heal, to Train, to Entertain. ...y-Séré won the 2000 Script Writing Award given ...Brooks Center of Chicago State University for her ...BO. In conjunction with that award, the play was first ...e 2001 edition of *Warpland: A Journal of Black Literature* ...umBO and the playwright's companion one-act play *Abiona* ...equently selected for an Illinois Arts Council Grant in support ...matic reading at the International House of the University of ...ago. Ms. Séré's plays have been performed in educational and ...ertainment programs at various other venues in the Chicago area.

Ms. Séré's plays have also been read and performed in workshops at the Actors Studio of New York City, as well as at the National Black Theater Festival of Winston-Salem, North Carolina.

Holding a Master's Degree in Social Work from the University of Illinois and a Master of Arts in English Language and Literature from the University of Chicago, Ms. Séré has had extensive social work and teaching experience at various private and public institutions. She is a member of the National Association of Social Workers and the Dramatists Guild of America.

CPSIA information can be obtained at www.ICGtesting.com
Printed in the USA
LVOW05s2133070214

372619LV00011B/50/P